# HIGH PRAISE FOR:
## JONATHAN VALIN

"In Cincinnati the territory belongs to Jonathan Valin." —*Time*

"Valin is . . . in the very small class of people who transcend the noble ghosts of Chandler and Hammett." —Peter Straub

"A superior writer . . . smart and sophisticated." —*The New York Times Book Review*

"Valin is obviously asking more of the detective formula than a vehicle for registering violent sensations so typical of mainline gumshoe storytelling; his interest is shifting to a deeper portrayal of ethical and metaphysical questions." —*Cincinnati Enquirer*

"An inveterate tilter at windmills . . . Valin is a writer drawn to serious stuff in general and moral issues in particular." —*Philadelphia Inquirer*

"One of the best of today's practitioners of the hard-boiled school . . . Valin has laid claim to the greater Cincinnati scene and it is his territory; no one else captures it as vividly or as darkly as he does." —*Cincinnati Post*

"Valin's strengths: crisp narration, perfect-pitch dialogue, quick-stroked descriptions, memorable supporting characters, and a hero-narrator with a distinctive voice and outlook." —*The Washington Post*

**Books by Jonathan Valin**

DAY OF WRATH
DEAD LETTER
EXTENUATING CIRCUMSTANCES
FINAL NOTICE
FIRE LAKE
LIFE'S WORK
THE LIME PIT
THE MUSIC LOVERS
NATURAL CAUSES
SECOND CHANCE

JONATHAN VALIN

# THE LIME PIT

A DELL BOOK

Published by
Dell Publishing
a division of
Bantam Doubleday Dell Publishing Group, Inc.
1540 Broadway
New York, New York 10036

ISBN: 0-440-21029-1

Printed in the United States of America

Published simultaneously in Canada

May 1994

10  9  8  7  6  5  4  3  2  1

OPM

TO KATHERINE

# 1

IT WAS A warm noon in early July. From my desk I watched a black-bodied wasp floating past the screen of the office window. He and a dozen or so of his cronies had built a hive on the sixth-floor cornice of the Riorley Building, directly below my office; and now, in the early summer heat, they circled and droned through the air in a lazy, rancorous cloud, like a little spot of bad weather in an otherwise flawless sky.

I had just gotten back to Cincinnati Thursday morning, after spending the better part of two days in Chicago, running down a con-man by the name of Aaron Mull. He was an interesting character, Mull—a kind of corn-belt Prospero who had tricked two realtors into parting with a large sum of cash. It was a beautiful scam and it could only have been run on the very greedy or the maladroit, which was why the two real estate men had looked so goddamn angry when they'd popped into my office on the first of the month. The taller and more imposing of the pair, a bug-eyed man named Leo Meyer, explained the situation in a hoarse, aggrieved voice, while his partner, Larry Cox, literally wrung his hands in rage. These were not-so-newly-rich men, used to getting their own ways in a world of cutthroat scheming. They had worked their way up (so Meyer told me) the "hard way," had "fought" for every penny that was theirs. And (so I told myself, though I didn't tell Meyer) it had taken this schemer, Aaron Mull, to summon up a history that had been, for a decade at least, buried under the loose earth of acquisitions—fine houses, fine cars, and the fine clothes, the tailored suits, the Brooks Brothers shirts and ties, the Bally shoes—that now seemed to Meyer mere figments from some dream of worldly happiness.

I took the case. Hell, why not? Meyer's self-righteousness may have been as phoney as Mull's scam and his usual business ethics just as questionable, but money is money, whoever has handled it. And, once in your hands, it's an orphan, a new limb waiting to be grafted green on the family tree.

I'd found Mull, all right. Working the same scam on a Northside Chicago realtor. And I'd turned him over to the police. Not without a tussle, however, because Aaron Mull was a crafty son-of-a-bitch and, like most imaginative men, a selfish one. In fact, when I finally caught up with him in the tar lot of a

Northside I.G.A., he denied he was Aaron Mull. And, for just a second, in the dry shimmering heat of that grocery parking lot, I believed him. Maybe it was the heat or maybe it was just another facet of that gift that made him so good at what he did, but, by God, in his checked short-sleeved shirt, his Levi's and Hush Puppies, with his shock of pale brown hair, his tan beardless face and huckleberry grin, he *didn't* look like an Aaron Mull. He backed away, smiling with just the right air of affronted good nature. And then I collared him.

Mull jerked away, and there followed a merry chase among the parked cars and abandoned grocery carts. I had to bash him one at the end of it—a hard tap across the noggin with my pistol, which really wasn't fair, as Mull pointed out when I cuffed him and called the police.

It was about midnight when the Chicago cops finished with me. The night was blessedly cool after the heat of the day and, rather than waiting for it to warm up again and driving in a sweat all the way back to Cincy, I walked over to the police lot, got in my Pinto and headed out Lake Shore to Stoney Island and from there to the Indiana toll road and the interstate that led to home. I stopped once at a Stuckey's outside of Indianapolis for a cup of coffee and an egg salad sandwich; and, while the waitress sauntered sleepy-eyed behind the counter and a handful of truckers, dressed in jeans and workshirts with openbacked CAT (for Caterpillar) caps on their heads, chatted and joked in one of the booths, I nursed my cup of coffee and watched the sunrise through the truck-stop window. I felt good. I'd done a good job. And, with the money I'd made from it, I could just keep driving on 65, all the way down through Kentucky, Tennessee, and Mississippi to the Gulf. It was a wonderful feeling of freedom that didn't last much longer than the moment it took me to reflect on how hot it would be on the Gulf and how little I liked driving through the swelter of July; but it was a feeling that very few people can afford to indulge in. Maybe the truckers at the nearby booth. And maybe the two real estate tycoons, whom I would call from my office that morning. You have to be god-awful rich or one of the chosen poor to entertain the illusion that your life is a matter of free choices. It's mostly an illusion, as Mull had found out. But it's a damn good feeling while it lasts. Almost worth a year to two in the slammer, which was all Mull would get as a first offender. And certainly worth the crap that *I* had to put up with daily.

I'd gotten into town at seven A.M. and, still exhilarated, driven straight to the Riorley Building. It wasn't until that noon, as I sat drowsing, feet up on the desk, staring at the cloud of wasps as if they were an omen, that the fatigue caught up with me and the excitement left me the way it leaves an active kid —in a sudden swoop, a downward spin that makes you wonder if there will ever be anything in the world worth getting *that* excited about again.

I was sitting in the diner, watching the sun rise

in a great purple aura above the horizon line of treetops and skeletal high-power stations, when the kitchen phone rang. The waitress was too tired to pick it up; and the truckers didn't seem to hear it. Baby-faced Aaron Mull, dressed in bib overalls and a collarless shirt, walked out of the kitchen and said, "I'm not going to answer it." Which left me. I reached across the lunch counter, but the space between the mushroom-shaped stools and the far wall was suddenly extended, and it was like reaching across the dead space toward the wild animals at a zoo. The phone kept ringing. And I kept reaching. And then I opened my eyes and I was back in the office, with a telephone buzzing insistently on my desk.

I picked it up.

"I want to speak to . . . Mister . . . Harold . . . Stoner," a high-pitched, whimsical voice said. The speaker was male, probably elderly; from the lacunae in his speech, the emphatic pauses between words, I imagined he was either a man who took himself very seriously or that he simply wasn't used to talking over the phone, wasn't sure the contraption would convey clearly the nuances of speech—like my own grandmother who used to yell into the receiver to be sure she would be heard over "all that distance."

I rubbed my eyes with my free hand and said: "This is Stoner speaking."

"Harold Stoner?"

I held the receiver away from my ear and looked at it. "Yes. This is Harold Stoner."

"My name is Cratz, Mr. Stoner. Hugo . . . Harold . . . Cratz. We got the same name."

"What can I do for you, Mr. Cratz?"

"It's not me," he said with a sorrowful catch in his voice. "It's my little girl, Cindy Ann. They done something to her."

And with that Hugo Cratz began to whimper—weak feminine sobs that made me shift uncomfortably in my chair. I let him have his cry over Cindy Ann—wife, daughter, granddaughter, whoever she was he had loved and lost. And when he'd finished, I told him to call the police, because I had the feeling that Hugo Cratz didn't need a private detective yet, just a friendly ear.

But he surprised me. "Shoot, I already been to the police. Goddamn fools try to tell me she's left town. I says to them, 'If she left town, how come she don't leave no word? How come that friend of hers, Laurie, is acting like she is?'

"Well?" Cratz said when I didn't speak up. "How come?"

"I don't know."

"You think you could find out?"

"I can try," I told him. "Come downtown to my office tomorrow. Say about nine-thirty. And fill me in on the details."

"Can't come downtown," Cratz said. "Had a stroke last year and I don't get around much any more, save for a walk in the park. You can come out here if you like. 2014 Cornell. First floor front."

I started to write down the address on a notepad. And then I put the pencil down. With what I had made from the Meyer deal I didn't need Hugo Cratz's money. Or the trouble he was bound to give me. Because Hugo Cratz was trouble. I didn't need any omens to tell me that. "Wouldn't you be better off waiting a couple of days," I said to him. "Maybe Cindy Ann *did* leave town. Maybe she'll be back in a couple of days."

"She's all I got," Cratz said weakly. "My little girl is all I got."

I picked up the pencil and scratched out the street number. It was in northside Clifton—a respectable address. "All right, Mr. Cratz. It'll cost you two hundred dollars a day plus expenses."

"Uh-huh," he said too quickly. "All right."

"You've got that kind of money?"

"Well, not just lying around, I don't," he said. "I can get it for you, though. In a couple of days. And as for those expenses . . . it don't cost but twenty-five cents to get from here to downtown on the Metro, and twenty-five cents back. So I don't figure that should amount to much."

"What if I have to spend a few days on the job, Mr. Cratz?"

He snorted. "With Laurie living right across the street! Hell, you can find out the right of this in half an hour. And that don't come to but eight dollars and thirty-three cents. Figuring twelve hours in a work day," he added.

I took a breath. "So you estimate between the bus fare and the half hour I'll be working for you that you'll owe me . . ."

"Eight dollars and eighty-three cents," Hugo Cratz said smartly. "And I'll have it for you in a couple of days."

I laughed out loud.

"Don't you believe me?" Cratz said. "Mister, I need your help. No matter what it costs, I need your help."

He needs my help.

What the hell? It was only a couple of miles out of my way, and I was going home anyway. And I'd made a big bundle for doing practically nothing. And I could afford to be charitable. And a little, quite unprofessional part of me—maybe the best part, all things considered—very much wanted to take a quick look at the man behind that stubborn whimsical voice.

"All right," I said. "I know I'm making a mistake, but I'm going to take you up on your deal, Mr. Cratz. One half hour's work. Pro-rated. I'll be out around three. And we'll see what we can do about finding your little girl."

# 2

NORTH CLIFTON IS one of the oldest suburbs of Cincinnati—a neighborhood of storied frame houses and spindle-railed verandas, of white-capped gaslights and maple-shaded lawns. It's picturesque and, like many picturesque neighborhoods, it has a chilling uniformity of character, as if the householders propped sternly in their lawn chairs or gazing out from the black space of a porch have been chosen and supplied to ornament their homes. It's not that the houses don't look lived in; on the contrary, Clifton looks thoroughly lived in, richly historical in the clutter and detail of everyday life. But it is a sedate and melancholy clutter that smacks of decay. Despite the contradictory evidence—the deserted bicycle blazing on a sunlit lawn, the bright yellow plastic truck abandoned on the sidewalk, and the occasional dart of a child's playful voice—I felt as I drove up Cornell that, like a bar or a graveyard, this was not a place for the young. Perhaps Cindy Ann Cratz had felt that way too.

Hugo Cratz lived six doors in from Ludlow in a three-story red frame house with a white slat veranda and a tall maple tree set in a modest yard. A hedge of rosebushes flowed about the veranda and continued back along the driveway to the rear of the house. Two old men were walking up the driveway when I pulled in. One of them had been burly once —big-shouldered and strong-armed. But he had shriveled away in his old age and now carried himself with a kind of sodden, humpbacked fatigue, as if it pained him slightly to move at all. His chest was caved in and showed, sallow and hairless, through the front of his checked shirt. The head above the chest was sharp-featured and crowned with a tonsure of wispy white hair. His chin, peppered with stubble, turned upward; his sharp nose turned down; so that his mouth ran like a thin dark crease between them. The other man was fat, nimble, and deeply tanned on the face and arms. He wore a tight yellow T-shirt that accentuated the sway of his gut and the fat paps that sagged above his belly. His face was square, pleasant, and considerably younger-looking than the other man's. I guessed that the frail one was Hugo Cratz, and I was right.

"Hello!" he called out, waving his arm as if it were as jointless as a stick. "You must be Stoner. Glad you could come out."

There was something of the planter's manner in

Cratz's voice, a Southern geniality that I'd missed over the phone. I figured he was putting it on for his big-bellied friend; and, oddly enough, it made Hugo come alive for me. That swagger was human. It fleshed him out, gave him the bulk he once must have had and a little of the athlete's vanity, that condescension that sportscasters and fans confuse with kindness. It put money in his loose khaki trousers, a wad of it tied with a rubber band. Blackened his hair and eye. Gave him a temper and a streak of mean parsimonious pride. Hugo Cratz, I decided, was probably a tough and devious old man.

"Let's sit and talk," he said when I'd walked to where he and his pal were standing. "Up on the porch."

There were two painted lawn chairs on the veranda and a big porch swing. Cratz took one chair, I took the other. And his friend sat on the top step of the stoop.

"George is O.K.," Cratz said, glancing down at the fat man. George raised his head and nodded seriously.

I glanced at the pack of Lucky Strikes that George had rolled in his shirt sleeve.

The poverty of some men's lives never fails to shake me. And, sitting on the porch, with George hunched affably below me and Hugo Cratz leaning intimately forward in his chair, I was suddenly conscious of just how much I represented in the way of excitement and novelty to those two old men. It made me feel like backing off that porch on tiptoe,

**11**

climbing in the car and driving straight home to the Delores. Instead, I squirmed and made small nods and tried to avoid looking into Hugo Cratz's juicy blue eyes as he reminisced, walking slowly through a maze of memories, establishing along the way his own credentials as a man, until he arrived again at that center space where his manhood failed—his daughter's, Cindy Ann's space—and he broke down in big tears. Even his friend George turned away then, though he must have heard it a dozen times before. And I . . . I stared out at the tired, sun-drenched street and thought what a fool I was to play detective with Hugo Cratz.

Cratz excused himself and walked into the apartment house to wipe his nose. I could see him through the first-floor bay window. There were plants in the bay—leafy asparagus ferns, begonias, and purple-leafed Wandering Jew. Either Cindy Ann had a pleasant domestic touch or Hugo Cratz was less the crusty played-out old man than he appeared to be.

"You've got to excuse him," fat George said suddenly in a low, unfriendly voice. "He just ain't been the same since that little bitch left him."

"You want to tell me about her, George?" I asked.

George looked quickly at the glass-frame door of the apartment building and took a deep noisy breath in through his nostrils.

"What do you want, mister?" he said hoarsely. "He don't have any money left, if that's what you want." George took another deep breath and his big chest heaved. "He ain't got nothing left," he said, looking down at the seams in the pavement. "Time was he wouldn't need me to say it for him."

I sat back in the lawn chair and tried manfully to look like a tough detective for slow, stubborn George. But the harder I tried, the more I felt as if my mail-order diploma were showing—the one with the machine guns on it. And after a moment or so, I realized that it wasn't only George who was making me feel like a boob. Something wasn't right. Whatever that something was, George considered it criminal, a pathetic by-product of Cratz's old age. And Cratz thought it was embarrassing and just too damn sad.

And then it came to me with a certainty that made me shiver in the hot July air. I shivered and then I blushed for Hugo, for George, and for myself. A chorus of cicadas started a shrill round in the nearby rosebushes, and I remembered the wasps outside my office window. That's what they were trying to tell you, Harry, I thought and laughed to myself. The cicadas grew shriller. The sunlight on the lawn glowed as whitely as a fluorescent bulb. I squinted and searched the yard for some evidence— some sunlit toy or sign of kinship. A yellowhammer drummed on a distant maple tree. Then the cicadas died down. A cloud passed across the lawn. And, in the hush, I asked myself *what are you going to do now?*

Cindy Ann——. Whatever it was, it wasn't *Cratz*. She wasn't his daughter, his granddaughter, his wife. She wasn't any relation at all. She was just a girl, probably poor-white from lower Vine, who had seen old Hugo as a stepping stone on the way out of tarboard shacks, poverty, and the old age that comes on almost overnight. She'd probably bilked the old man out of a few dollars or a few Social Security checks. And then went on her merry way. And Hugo, Hugo Cratz, the man I was working for, who had loved the little gold-digger with that shameless, impotent infatuation that age has for youth . . . Hugo Cratz was just a very sentimental, very lonely, and very *dirty* old man.

"It's not a bad place," Hugo said as he reseated himself on the lawn chair. Frail as he was and wet-eyed, he looked like a fuzzy-haired, wizened child. "My son's got a nicer one up in Dayton. Nice boy, Ralph. He'll send me the money. I mean if it ends up costing me a few dollars to find her." Cratz surveyed the lawn and said again, "It's not a bad place. Schwartz bought it for his kids seven, eight years ago, when old man Carroll died. He divided it up good. Split the downstairs into eight measly apartments. Then jacked up the rent so's I had to take the job of handyman just to stay on. It was a helluva lot of work for me alone. 'Course with Cindy Ann around there wasn't much to it. She'd take care of the lawn and I'd look after the garbage and repairs." Hugo's eyes began to tear and his thin collapsed mouth trembled. "It was real nice," he said.

"She's no kin of yours, is she, Mr. Cratz?" I said softly. "No blood relative?"

Cratz ducked his head, and I caught sight of George fidgeting uncomfortably on the stoop.

"What if she isn't?" Cratz said defiantly. "Does a person have to be kin for you to care about 'em, to want to make sure they're all right?"

"What if she doesn't want to be taken care of?"

"What're you saying?" Cratz said slowly. Anger dried his blue eyes and gave his thin face a sharp, predatory vigor.

"All I'm saying is what the police have probably already told you. If Cindy Ann left you of her own free will, there's absolutely nothing you can do about it. You can't hire someone to make her come back to you, Mr. Cratz, as much as you might want to."

Cratz made a shrill little noise in the back of his throat—a stifled scream. Then he grabbed me savagely by the arm. "C'mon," he said, pulling me out of the chair toward the apartment door. "C'mon in here. And you—" he pointed at George, "get on home. Goddamn loudmouth," he said under his breath.

George started to say something in his own defense, but Hugo cut him off with a chop of his left hand. "Can it, George. I blame myself. I shoulda known better than to leave you out here with this one." He plucked me by the sleeve. "And don't you say nothing neither. This is *my* time we're on now. And I already used up two and one-half dollars of it lollygagging."

He shoved me through the door into a dark,

musty antechamber. On the right a stairwell coiled up to the second floor; on the left a narrow hallway meandered toward the rear of the house. Cratz walked down the hallway to the first door on the right and fumbled in his pants pocket for a key.

"I always keep it locked," he said. "Two years ago we had some niggers move in on the second floor. 'Bout then apartments started getting broken into." Cratz cackled dryly. "I'd like to see 'em break in here. Yes, I would. After you," he said, pushing the door open.

The door frame was low and I had to stoop to make it through.

"You're pretty good size, ain't you?" Cratz said with a touch of expertise. "What d'you go? 'Bout six-three? 'Bout two-twenty?"

"Two-fifteen," I said, surveying the dim little room. Cratz's apartment looked to be no bigger than a small storeroom and it was stuffed like a storeroom with sprung and faded furnishings.

"You ever play ball?" Cratz asked me.

"Some. In college."

"What? End, maybe?"

"You got it."

Cratz chuckled. "Don't mind the mess. Just sit yourself down."

There was a television whispering on my left on a flecked metal trolley and a big scarred darkwood table in the shallow bay. A chair covered with a torn and dusty yellow throw sat next to the table, and a sprung, pea-green convertible couch next to the chair. The bed was pulled open; and the sheets were rumpled and dirty. Behind the couch was a stone mantle crowded with photos of a young man in uniform. Beyond the couch the narrow room emptied abruptly into an alcove the size of a small walk-in closet. In it were a long trough-shaped sink and a tiny Kelvinator refrigerator that made a mournful, ubiquitous hum. The apartment was so narrow that the front of the convertible bed actually touched the credenza stacked against the far wall. The walls themselves were papered in a faded, water-stained stripe that was peeling off near the ceiling. The whole place stank of grease, old clothing, and unwashed flesh.

"It ain't much, is it?" Cratz confessed as he sank down on the open bed. "I just said that stuff about it being a nice place to comfort that old woman George." He looked about the room with a mournful, watery eye. "No, it ain't much to show after seventy-some years."

"About George," I said, sitting gingerly on the dusty edge of the yellow chair. "He didn't say a word about Cindy Ann."

"Then how'd you know?"

"I guessed. It wasn't too hard to guess from the way you were acting."

Cratz stared out the big window at the bright expanse of lawn. "It's dark in here, ain't it?" he said softly. "I gotta replace that overhead bulb. 'Course it's hard for me to get up on a ladder since I had the stroke. It done something to my sense of balance.

Man, I used to be as light-footed as a cat." Hugo toed the faded rug and looked over at me. "I know it's shameful. To be so old and so damn helpless. I know it. I know that's what you're thinking, too. You get to a certain age and people, younger folks, figure you're through with life. You ain't even supposed to have an appetite any more—just pick at your food and smile. 'Bout now it's all supposed to wind down. And you're supposed to get yourself all prepared for the big one. Like starving yourself a little at a time out of all the pleasures of life was the way of easing into it. Don't you believe it! I ain't prepared to die. I wake up in a cold sweat every night thinking of it. Stuff the damn sheet in my mouth to keep from crying out." Cratz pressed a hand over the crumpled sheets. "But, then, she'd be there," he said, patting the mattress. "And I'd feel better.

"You know where Mt. Storm Park is?"

I nodded.

"It ain't so far from here. And up to the time of my stroke I could walk it easy. Just cut down Mount Olive and over to the Park Road. Me and George used to go over there every damn afternoon. Just to be doing something. That's where I met her, Cindy Ann. Stretched out on a beach blanket alongside the shelter house. Man," Cratz said wistfully, "she was a sight. And pleasant to me. Not thinking right off what maybe she should have been thinking. That I was just another old man looking down her sun dress. Which I was, too. No, she was too sweet for that. We started to chat and she invites me to sit down. And I told George I wouldn't be needing him any further. And that's how I spent that afternoon until way on toward sunset, sitting on that big yellow beach towel of hers and telling her about my life.

"It ain't often that you can find a young person that you can sit and talk to. They just don't care about the past. But Cindy Ann was different. And it wasn't like she was putting on. Boy, you get old enough and you can spot that sort of thing a mile away. She cared about me. Maybe having come from a broken home and being miles away from it and her folks and her friends she needed somebody to care for. So I'd walk on out to that park every day. And she'd be there waiting. And it got so that was the only thing I'd look forward to in the day. Sitting with Cindy Ann in the park and telling her about my days in the Corps or about football or my son. Whatever.

"And then one day 'bout a year ago, I come to the park and she wasn't there. Man, I'd liked to die. I didn't know what happened to her. Whether she was hurt or sick or something worse. I got George to lend me his car and I spent the whole damn afternoon driving through Clifton, just looking to see if I could catch sight of her. I come home, feeling like an old man, and, damn, if she wasn't setting out there on that very stoop waiting for me! I ain't ever seen anything looked as good as that little girl sitting on the stoop, with her little bag of clothes and things in her hand.

"To this day I don't know why she come to me. I just figured she needed a place to stay and I offered her the couch and she said, Yes, O.K., for a while.

"We had a real good year together, mister. A real good year. And, right off, I made her promise me that if she ever wanted to leave she would tell me first. So's I wouldn't spend another afternoon like I did when she didn't show up in the park. And she promised. *That's* how come I know something's happened to her. She never said goodbye, and Cindy Ann would never've done me that way. She was good to me. Looking after me. Cleaning up this hole."

Cratz began to cry, tears rolling down his cheeks and dropping heavily to the rug. "Ain't supposed to fall in love at my age," he said. "Ain't supposed to care too much. Too near the end. Too near the grave. Mistake, maybe." He swallowed hard and swiped at his red nose. "You see, I didn't force her to do nothing. She come of her own free will, like you said. And I just . . . I just ain't got enough . . . it ain't fair they should've taken her from me." Cratz began to sob. "It ain't fair."

"Who are 'they,' Mr. Cratz?"

*"Them!"* he said ferociously and pointed to the window. "Them! Them! Them damn heartless bastards that called themselves her friends. That's who!"

# 3

**I KNEW WHAT** she'd say before she said it. I knew because I knew that Hugo was a tired man at the end of his own particular road. Maybe I just wanted to hear her say it, so that I could tell myself I'd given the old man his full half-hour's worth. Maybe if Laurie B. Jellicoe had lived on Lorraine or Newman, instead of two houses down on the opposite side of Cornell, I would have called it a mistaken afternoon. Mistakes happen. Hugo Cratzs happen, although we don't usually see them unless they're selling newspapers in front of a rusted tarbarrel on a windy street corner. Maybe if it hadn't been so sleepy hot that I had to pack my sportscoat over my sleeve like a waiter's napkin, I'd have been thinking more clearly about Hugo Cratz. Maybe I'd have seen him for the bigoted reprobate that he was. Using his devils and his debilities to perpetuate the myth of one Cindy Ann *X*. Who, judging from the dogeared photograph that Cratz had shown me before I went a-hunting, was probably fell and feeble-minded. Blonde-haired, buck-toothed, sixteen-year-old girlchild with a thin, pale, avaricious face. Who was probably five states away by now on the back of a motorcycle, hanging on for dear life to the belt of whichever rambler she had spotted at Reflections or the Dome and taken a liking to. Probably.

But all I was thinking about that late July afternoon, as I trudged through the maple trees up to the two-story brownstone apartment house that Cratz had designated with trembling hand—as if he were pointing to Gehenna and the altar of Baal—was that old man's apartment and the old man smells of ripe, unimpeded decay. There were nights when my own rooms smelled of the same death that Hugo was trying to lie his way out of. And, after hearing his story and seeing the way he lived, I just didn't have it in me to tell him it was a hopeless cause.

So I trudged across the street and up the concrete pathway of 1309 and into the blue-tiled lobby with its brass mailboxes set in stippled yellow plaster and ran my finger across the name slots until I came to *Jellicoe*. Number Four. I walked up to the second landing and, either from force of habit or simply from the sheer contrast with Cratz's place, noted the swirl of detergent on the freshly mopped floors, the woodlight sheen of the balustrade, and the framed print of a sailing ship hung in the hall. It was a nice, expensive little apartment house and Laurie B. Jellicoe—when she answered the door—seemed a nice, smart-looking young woman.

"Yes?" she said in a breathy, little girl voice. "Can I help you?"

I took a good look at her and balked. Tall, about twenty-five, dressed tastefully out of Cardin, with a blonde, bland Farrah-Fawcett face and a great mane of ash-blonde hair, Laurie Jellicoe looked like the last person on earth who would have befriended a gamine like Cindy Ann.

"Well?" she said.

"Well—" I said. "You're a nice-looking girl."

She nodded almost imperceptibly.

"I guess that's not news."

"What is it you want?" she said with an edge in her voice. "If you're selling anything—"

"No, I'm not selling. I'm working for Hugo Cratz. I'm a private detective."

Laurie Jellicoe's eyes widened and her arm slithered down the door like a snake gliding down a tree trunk. "I don't believe it!" she barked with laughter. "He hired a private detective?"

I reddened a little.

"Hey, Lance," Laurie called over her shoulder to someone sitting in the living room. "Old man Cratz hired a private cop. Can you believe that!"

There was a terrific creak, like the sound of a tank shifting onto its tracks, and then a pound, pound, pound that shook the floorboards. The door flew open and Lance, all ten feet of him in a T-shirt with a "have a nice day" face on it, blue jeans, cowboy boots that curled at their tips like a witch's toes, blocked the light. Laurie Jellicoe patted him proprietarily on the butt and said, "Easy there, baby," in a low jocund voice.

Lance was a sandy-haired giant, a long-nosed, square-jawed, big-chinned Texas boy. Men his size don't come along all that often; and I realized as I stood in his shadow that I had seen him once before in the University Plaza at the corner of Vine and McMillan, striding across the arcade toward the Nautilus Health Club. I was buying cigarettes at Walgreen's at the time, and ol' Lance had practically emptied the rear of the store in his wake. Shopgirls and lady customers had plastered themselves against the window to watch him pass. "What a hunk!" one of the shopgirls said to a girlfriend, who whistled soft agreement.

In the flesh, Lance was a mean-looking hunk, with one of those vain, stupid, pretty-boy faces that get very tough and very shrewd around the eyes.

"You say you're working for that tired piece of shit?" he said in a low Southern baritone. "What kind of man would earn his living like that? No kind of man I'd like to know."

"Why'd you ask, if you already knew the answer?"

Lance took a breath and, I swear, I could hear the elastic threading of his T-shirt pop.

"Go back inside, honey," Laurie said quickly. "I'll handle this."

Ol' Lance gave me one helluva angry look and plunged a finger the size of a dollar cigar at my chest. "Be seeing you," he said sharply. He managed to pack enough real menace into those three words to make me think twice before I ever wised off to him again. He patted Laurie on the rear and rumbled back into the living room.

Laurie watched him retreat and then turned to me. "Mister," she said in that little girl voice. "You don't know how close you came."

"I think, maybe, I have an idea."

"No, you don't," she said. She gave me an appreciative look, a cold professional sizing-up, and smiled favorlessly. "He'd squash you like a bug."

I hadn't realized it before—the clothes, the little girl good looks, and the timid breathy voice had disguised it—but this Laurie was a hunk herself. Big-boned, big-breasted, with long handsome legs and a firm round rear that showed seamlessly beneath her tailored slacks, she made a good match for ol' Lance. I couldn't help thinking she made a good match, period. She caught that look in my eye—girls that are built like she was never miss it—and shook her head, no.

"Don't even think about it," she said with a cautionary grin.

"Can't kill a man for dreaming."

"You don't know Lance." She glanced quickly into the living room. "Another place, another life, maybe it'd be different."

"I'll take that as a compliment," I said.

"What is it that Cratz expects you to find out?" Laurie Jellicoe said, leaning back against the door. "Where we stashed Cindy Ann?"

I nodded. "That's it."

She didn't say anything for a second. Just stared at me with a mild worry in her stone-blue eyes. "Look, Mr.—"

"Stoner. Call me Harry."

"Look, Harry," she said. "In the last couple of days we've had the police here two times. Cratz has called us every hour on the hour since Monday. And we're just a little sick and tired of the whole thing. I wish to God at this point that I'd never met the girl."

"You two were friends?"

Laurie Jellicoe shrugged. "Yeah, I guess so. We did laundry together down on Ludlow and we'd go shopping at Keller's together. To tell you the truth, I think she had a crush on Lance." Laurie passed a tan hand through her golden hair. "I felt sorry for her. Coming from a broken home. Having to live the way she did. She was one of those runaway kids who you just know are going to end up in trouble. She had that victim look about her. You know? So washed-out that her eyes were the only color in her face. And skinny. And just as awkward and naive as hell. In a way she was lucky, tying up with Cratz. At least he didn't abuse her physically. Not that he wouldn't have if he'd been able to." Laurie Jellicoe grimaced. "He's such an awful old man. Dirty and repulsive. It was no wonder she couldn't take it anymore—living over there. Especially after his stroke. Cleaning up his messes. Practically feeding him by hand. It gives me the fantods to think about it," she said with a shudder.

"Fantods?"

"Just a word that my grandma used to use." Laurie smiled half-heartedly. "You know I've told this to the police. Do you really want me to go through it again?"

"Please."

"All right. Last Sunday Cindy Ann came over here to talk. She told me that she'd found a guy—I don't know who. Some biker in Norwood who worked days at the General Motors assembly plant. She'd met him at a V.F.W. dance that Cratz had sent her off to and she'd just gone crazy over him. And, now, she didn't know what to do about the old man. I never did understand why she cared for him. But there must have been something decent about Cratz, because she didn't want to leave him in the lurch. She came to me to talk it out. Girl to girl, you know? She was such a pathetic little thing, and she always looked up to me like I was some sort of, you know, authority. Because of Lance and all. Well, we talked and she said she was afraid that Cratz would get steamed if he knew that she was running off with a young guy. He was very jealous in that way. So, I suggested that she tell him she was going home to see her folks and that she was going to spend the night before she left with us. You see Lance has a car and she could say that he planned to drive her down to the bus station around midnight. I mean it wasn't that unusual. She'd stayed overnight before to listen to music and just to talk. So, she told Cratz what she was going to do and came over here on Sunday night. About eleven or so some kid rode up on a chopper and Cindy Ann left with him. She told me before she left that if Cratz asked about her to tell him that she'd be in touch when she could. And she cried a little. And we hugged and kissed each other. And that was it."

"That's the last time you saw her?"

Laurie nodded. "Cratz thinks we've made off with her. I guess that's partly my fault for con- cocting that cock and bull story about her folks. Somehow he managed to get their number in Sioux Falls or wherever the hell she was from. And they hadn't heard from her and weren't interested in hearing. Some family, huh? So he called the cops and told them we'd kidnapped her! Can you believe it! On Monday morning a fat little man showed up and started asking all kinds of questions about the 'alleged' Cindy Ann. Eventually we figured out what was going on and told him the whole story, just like I'm telling you. But that wasn't good enough for Cratz. He's a sick old man. Sick in the head. That stroke must have really addled his brains. On Tues- day he called the cops again. And he hasn't quit calling them or us since. Our life is really getting to be a mess. Both Lance and I were late to work on Monday and Tuesday and, of course, having police cars pull up in front of your house is really good public relations. And, now, he's hired you!"

"Laurie!" Lance boomed from the living room.

"Look," Laurie said breathily. "I gotta go before there's trouble. Be a good guy, will you, and tell Cratz the truth? *Make* him believe it. Please. I gotta go."

She ducked quickly into the living room and closed the door.

＝＝＝＝＝

It was almost six o'clock when I finished with Laurie Jellicoe. Outside of Lance, there'd been no surprises. She'd told me exactly what I'd expected to hear and left me with the distasteful job of convincing Hugo Cratz that Cindy Ann was gone for good.

Eight and one half dollars sure buys a lot of your time, Harry, I thought as I walked back beneath the maple trees and waited at the street corner for a white-haired woman to maneuver a Dodge station wagon into a narrow driveway. But I'd known what I was letting myself in for when I'd driven out to North Clifton that afternoon. I'd made a rich, easy buck off of Meyer and Cox, and I'd needed a Hugo Cratz to balance the books. That's all there was to it. A case of conscience. I get one every six months or so, after a particularly ugly or particularly easy job; and I hire myself out for charity work, to assuage that old monster inwit. Hugo was going to settle the account for a long, long time to come.

He was waiting for me on the porch, looking red-eyed and haggard and eager to hear what Laurie Jellicoe had told me. I supposed that he thought I'd backed her into a corner and beaten the truth out of her. A neat trick with ol' Lance standing around. But Cratz didn't seem suprised when I reported to him, word for word, what Laurie had actually said. He just shook his head and said, "You believe that crap?"

I bit the bullet and said, "Yes."

Hugo sat back in his porch chair and meditated a moment. "What if I was to tell you that I was watching Laurie's house from the time Cindy Ann left here until first light Monday morning and didn't see nobody on no bicycle drive up?"

"*Are* you telling me that?"

"I am."

I sighed. "Then I'd have to tell you that I don't believe you, Hugo. What possible reason would Laurie Jellicoe have to kidnap Cindy Ann?"

"They was using her," he said smugly. "For their damn sex orgies, is why."

"You're reaching, Hugo."

"Am I?" he said mildly. "Just you wait out here for a second."

He went into the house and came out about two minutes later with a tan shoebox under his arm. "You got a good look at that Laurie whilst you was in there?"

I nodded.

"Nice-looking woman, ain't she?" Hugo said and

smiled a sickly, broken-toothed smile. "Why'd you think I sent you over there? Think I was expecting you to get past that tree she keeps in the living room?"

"You mean Lance?" I said, feeling damn uncomfortable about this sudden coyness. A crafty Hugo Cratz was a different item than the grief-stricken, sentimental old man I'd foolishly committed myself to. I'd known he was devious when I'd first talked to him on the phone; but it had seemed such a transparent, clumsy sort of trickery that I hadn't really given it another thought. This new twist bothered me. For just a second I had the sickening feeling that Hugo Cratz had been using me since the moment we'd met.

"You take a look in there," he said, handing me the shoebox.

I tipped the lid and looked inside. There was still enough daylight in the western sky to make out the face of the girl in the photographs. It was Cindy Ann's face. I didn't look through them all. There was a tragic sameness about each one. They were Polaroids—SX70s—taken, most of them, in room light; some of them by a flash that had made Cindy Ann's naked blue eyes glow a demonic red. She didn't have much of a body, Cindy Ann. Her ribs and sharp hipbones were clearly visible in the photos. Her small girlish breasts already sagged like little pockets on her white chest. There were hands in most of the snapshots, reaching at her, caressing her, gouging her. Smooth red-tipped hands, chunky hairy ones. Holding cigarettes, clothespins, safety pins in one. And through it all Cindy Ann wore a bewildered, glassy-eyed smile. Staring straight into the camera, oblivious to the pain, she looked as properly posed as if a studio photographer had instructed her to look up and say, "Cheese." I slapped the lid on the box and shoved it back at Cratz. He was still smiling his sick, factitious smile.

"Where'd you get them?" I said hoarsely.

"Found 'em. After she left."

"Why the hell didn't you show them to me right away?" I said, as the anger hit me. A jolt of adrenaline that made me bite down hard and pound hard at the arm of the rusted lawn chair. "What kind of game are you playing, old man?"

"Didn't know if I could trust you," he said. "Wanted you to see them first. The two of them. Listen to their lies. Let them know you were listening. Same crap they told the police."

"Did you show these"—I pointed to the box—"to the police?"

Cratz knitted his brow savagely and looked at me with genuine disappointment. "I *love* her," he said through his teeth. "You got that, boy-o? You think I'd go showing them kind of pictures to men I don't trust? Anyway, those two'd just claim they didn't know nothing about them. Don't take but twenty-some dollars to buy one of those cameras. And I got one more reason. I don't want them bastards to know. I don't want to take no chances till I got

Cindy Ann back home with me. They find out I got them pictures, they might get antsy, do something foolish. I can't take that chance."

"So . . ." I said, letting out a deep, amazed breath. "You tricked me, Hugo."

"I did," he said. "I did indeed."

He smiled shyly and wet his lips. "Thought I was a blabbering cry-baby, didn't you? That's what ol' George thinks. He hates Cindy Ann for it, too. Thinks she's made a fool out of me. He can think what he damn well wants to. Point is I *know* what's going on. Them two are doing some awful things up in that apartment. She dresses so fine and he's such a looker, it ain't no wonder that Cindy Ann got messed up with them. I don't blame her none. Hell, I couldn't give her no love like that even if I could still get it up. Never felt that way about her after that first day in the park. I just wanted you to know that I'm no fool. I didn't spend some twenty years in the Corps and come out a coward. I can whine for the folks and play it as silly as they want. It ain't *all* show. Not by half. I start thinking about them photographs and it tears me up inside. But I wanted you to know—after I got a look at you and figured you was all right—that you can count on me.

"No police," he cautioned. "I just called them to throw a scare into them two. Let 'em know somebody's watching them. I want this done on the sly. And I want them bastards to get what's coming to them. And I don't *ever* want nobody to know what they done to my little girl. Is it a deal?"

I didn't really think about it. I wasn't in a thinking mood. Which is no way to run a business as perilous and actuarial as mine. Those photographs had touched a nerve, right down to the root, awakened the strict moralist who hides inside me and makes cheap ironic patter at the expense of my clients. Like an insult comedian, he's a sentimentalist, quick with the apologies, the gush about how all his needling is well-meant; and, like the insult comedian, his apologies are as phoney as his laughter. All he really understands is anger—a comprehensive anger that extends to anything that falls short of the ideal. Which is why he stays hidden most of the time. He's a vehement, childish cynic—all moralists and comedians are; and, in a different city, in a line of work less likely to give him occasion to rail, he'd probably get me into a lot of fights. But if Cincinnati is good for anything, it's good for beating the dickens out of a latent Puritan. There are too many of the real articles walking around. Too many of them with too much power. You can't beat a real Cincinnati moralist for cheap, stomach-turning sentimentality. I like this city; it keeps me sane.

But it's in my blood, too. And, sitting on that porch, pretending that banalities like idyllic childhood and the beauty of youth were as real as the chair I was sitting on, I was all Cincinnati Puritan, and as mad and vindictive as I could be. The Jellicoes gave me a royal case of the fantods. They made me nervous and sick at heart. Whether Cindy Ann had *wanted* to join their little circus, whether she'd be willing to give it up, didn't matter to me at that moment. All I wanted to do was to see that they got what was coming to them. And that Hugo got his "little girl" back.

"Yes," I said to Hugo Cratz. "It's a deal."

# 4

**WE SAT ON** the porch for another half hour, watching the daylight fail and listening to the pigeons on the skirts of the roof burble and coo. And, eventually, the detective in me began to ask his questions, a schoolboy's questions filled with whos and whys and wherefores.

By nightfall I had a reasonable understanding of the events leading up to the disappearance of Cindy Ann Evans—her last name was Evans, Hugo told me. I found out that it wasn't unusual for the girl to spend time with the Jellicoes or to sleep over at their tidy apartment. On that score, Laurie Jellicoe had been telling me the truth. Only the girl had never been gone for more than a night and had always left word with Hugo about when she'd be coming back home. Which meant that Laurie Jellicoe hadn't been telling the whole truth. And, as it turned out, neither had Hugo Cratz.

Hugo *had* seen someone leave the apartment house during his all-night vigil. The Jellicoes' yellow van had driven off around six on Sunday night and returned at seven the next morning. Whether Cindy Ann had been in it when it left or when it came back, Hugo couldn't say.

"They unloaded the damn thing in the lot behind the house," he said crankily. "If I'd a'had any gumption, I would a'gone on over there the minute I seen 'em come up the driveway."

"Gumption," I said to him, "is one of the things you *don't* have to worry about."

He chuckled drily. "You know, it's a strange thing about them two. They just don't seem to be around all that much. That's what first got me to thinking that something was wrong. That and the way Cindy Ann would look when she got home." He put a wrinkled hand to his mouth and lowered his voice, just like we were two old men sharing secrets on a park bench. "Think she might have been smoking some of that marijuana. Had a dazed eye, sometimes. Talked slurred, too. Had marks on her arms."

Great, I said to myself. An addict as well as a prostitute. Some Jellicoes.

"You said the two of them were out of their apartment a lot?"

"More than a lot." He nodded toward the building. "From what I seen they're in there maybe a couple-three days a week."

"Do you know where they go when they're not at home?"

He shook his head. "I heard Cindy Ann talking to them on the phone a couple of times. And she'd say, 'Frankfort!' or 'Lexington!' like it was a real pleasant suprise to her. I figure Kentucky is where they do their business, but it seems to be all over the state, like they was travelin' salesmen, selling . . ."

His mouth began to tremble again. I patted his arm.

"We don't know what they're selling, yet, Hugo. It could be just the pictures."

"Could, could it?"

He shook his head sadly. "I thought I'd seen it all. Been through wars. Been in a few dirty places. But this"—he patted the shoebox—"this just ain't human. How could they do a child like that?"

"Hugo," I said, feeling the end of that bad day in my bones. "I've given up asking that question—how could they? It just can't be answered. Give them both enough of a grudge against the world to make them users, manipulators trying to live out their childhood hurts on other children, and you can understand as much about the Jellicoes as can be understood."

"I guess," he said. "Only I ain't got that much charity in me." He looked at me expectantly. "So, I guess you'll get on top of them, now . . . now that you know how things stand?"

"I would have," I said. "But, thanks to your little trick, they know who I am, which means that the next time I see them, I want to be able to make more than vague accusations."

"Well, you could still follow them, couldn't you?" Hugo said irritably. And, suddenly, I had the certain knowledge that Hugo Cratz not only intended to hire me, he intended to run me, too.

"The way I see it, following them would be a very long and expensive proposition, with no guarantee at the end of it that we'd come up with Cindy Ann. We're lucky, in a sense. We have a piece of hard evidence. Let's make the most of those pictures. Let's find out where they came from and who they were meant for."

"Came from the Jellicoes," he said with disgust.

"Seems likely. But they may not be the only folks involved. And it's no good going into a game without knowing your competition."

"Pressure 'em," Hugo said, wringing Lance's neck with his hands.

"I'll do this my way, Hugo," I said with about as much firmness as I could command. "You went to a lot of trouble conning me into this deal. Don't blow the good will by telling me my job."

"Sorry. Sorry." He let go of Lance's throat and threw up his hands in apology. "Won't happen again."

Sure, I said to myself. And it won't be hot tomorrow, either.

I got to my feet. "I have to get some sleep."

"You'll come out here tomorrow?"

I told him I would. In the evening.

A big harvest moon—the size of a blood-red sun —was hanging above the maple trees on Cornell Avenue.

"Bodes fair weather," Hugo said.

He started for the apartment house door.

" 'Course I've known it to be wrong," he called out in a grim voice. And I knew he was thinking of his "little" girl and what the moon boded for her.

———

"Lance and Laurie Jellicoe."

I said their names aloud as I walked to the car.

What a sweet, chiming ring they had, a sweet and improbable pairing. How thoroughly and excusably middle-class they'd seemed in their smug little apartment with its picture of a sailing ship on the wall. Too fundamentally decent for something like this business. Only that was the moralist again, popping up in his sentimental garb. What better disguise for pornographers than solid Republican decency, I asked myself. And when it comes down to it, what criminal isn't middle-class in fact or aspiration? It could be the definition of a thief.

Well, I'd find out more about their business in the morning. I'd make the rounds of the local smut shops—the half-dozen storefronts on the north side of the city. Perhaps a clerk would recognize Cindy Ann's face, or, better still, I might find that face being pandered in one of the shop windows. If my luck held true, I might even be able to work my way back through the dealer to the Jellicoes' place of business or to the girl herself. On the other hand, if the photos were meant for sale, if nobody recognized the girl, then I could be sure that the Jellicoes were using them as advertisements. Which would be bad for Hugo and bad for his little girl, because what they advertised was a very rough trade indeed.

Adult News was the fourth shop I visited that hot Friday morning, and the only thing that distinguished it from the first three was the fact that its front window was painted red rather than green. The storefront was situated on the verge of the Vine Street tenderloin at the corner of Twelfth, next to a Pentecostal church, which, I suppose, should count for something when it comes to distinguishing features. I'm sure it counted for something to the Pentecostalists, three of whom were standing in the doorway of the church damning every customer that went into or came out of Adult News.

I tried my best to look saved as I walked past them. But judging from the frowns on their faces, I don't think they were convinced. The roadside to perdition must be crowded with such faces—lean and pitiless and full of smoke.

An unpainted square in the center of the smut shop window served as a teaser to passers-by. Behind it, a corkboard was posted with two dozen tame, unattractive nudes. And one of them was Hugo's Cindy Ann, reclining on a white cushion. She looked a bit more sophisticated in the Adult News photograph than she had in the ones I'd seen the night before—her face was carefully made up and she'd thrown her chest out, what little there was of it, and sucked in her round tummy like a professional model. Looking at her on display, I felt a wave of indignation rock me again. And I had to remind myself that it was a job and that there were unpredictable folks involved and that getting mad again wasn't going to help Hugo or his little girl.

I bent forward to the glass and peered closely at the face, just to be sure. Then I went inside the shop.

There was a tall glass display case to the right of the door. Behind it a very black Negro with a gold chain around his neck and teeth and eyes of the same color gold was leaning against a shiny register, gazing at his reflection in the chrome.

"What is it?" he said abstractedly. He tore himself away from his favorite sight and looked sullenly down at me.

"Those pictures in the window, are they for sale?"

"Sho'. Everything's for sale, man. Which one you want?"

"Lower left. There's a snapshot of a red-haired girl."

He turned to the window. The corkboard on which the photos were pinned swung open like a dutch door and a chunk of bright sunlight fell into the room. The black squinted at it furiously, as if it were a big yellow brick someone had tossed through his window.

"Which, now?" he said irritably.

I leaned over the counter and pointed to Cindy Ann.

He plucked the photograph off the cork and slammed the display door shut. "Man," he said, holding the picture at arm's length. "Can't say she do nothing for me." He slapped the photo to the glass. "Two dollars."

"Got any more like that one?" I said, pulling my billfold out.

"Could be. Got a whole box of them in the back there." He grinned. "Ah'll hold this one for you, suh, while you go'n take a look."

"You won't sell it to anyone while I'm gone?"

The black man looked at me stupidly.

I had the rear of the shop more or less to myself. It was dry-walled into a three-sided cube, racked on each side with magazines. A curtained portal in the back wall led to the peep shows, and there was a bin marked "Special" in the center of the floor. I rummaged through the torn magazines and snapshots inside the bin and came up with two more of Cindy Ann. Both of them were tame, nondescript Polaroids—very different fare from what Hugo had discovered in that shoebox. Which puzzled me.

I looked back up to the counter and decided it was time to do a little detection. After thinking it over, I decided a twenty dollar bill would be just about the right tool.

The clerk was staring at his own reflection again when I walked back up to the register. "Find what you looking for?" he said to me.

Some of them are back-slappers and some of them handle you as daintily as teacups. This one was the cautious type. But I figured that most of his suspiciousness came from being black and poor. Which made the twenty dollar bill seem more and more like a good idea. Besides, that gold in his eye wasn't all eyestrain.

"These pictures," I said in my most casual manner. "I'd like to get some more of them."

"You would?" he said, mocking my tone of voice. "How bad?"

I slipped the twenty out of my wallet.

"That bad?" he said and his eyes glittered. "Well, I'll tell you, we get us a shipment every month."

I started to put the bill back in my pocket when he reached out and grabbed my arm.

" 'Course you in a hurry. So you might try up to Gem Distributors on Mohawk."

He pulled the twenty out of my hand. "You can jus' keep them," he said, pointing to the three photographs. "They's your change."

———

It took me half an hour to walk up to Mohawk. Half an hour in the noon sun through that part of the city where commerce dies off and languishes in two-story storefronts and red-brick tenements. Used furniture stores, redneck bars with names like "Liberty Bell," two-dollar-a-day hotels, pawn shops, abandoned movie houses. Most great cities trail their own death around with them and sleep, like

John Donne, with one foot in the coffin. And the Over-the-Rhine, around Mohawk, is Cincinnati's dead-end.

It took me ten more minutes to find Gem Distributors, because, like a box within a box, Gem Distributors was tucked away inside an old white trolley depot. At least, it looked like it had been a trolley depot from the size of the round picket doors set in the white stone facade. I found a customer's entrance on the west side of the building and walked in. Two men were sitting on a dolly by the door, drinking wine from a paper bag. One of them had long red hair and the lush, simpering face of a painted Cupid. The other was older, with a great shock of white hair and white walrus moustaches and spry gray eyes. They were both a little drunk and, from the looks on their faces, I'd walked in on them in the middle of a joke. The old one got to his feet and dusted at his overalls, while Cupid broke up in laughter.

"Don't mind him, mister," the old one said. But there was laughter in his voice, too, and he was having a hard time containing it. He made his face over into a mask of seriousness. And the young one fell back on the dolly and roared.

"Shut up, Terry," the old one said. "Don't mind him, mister. What can I do for you?"

"I want to speak to the manager," I said.

"You're looking at him." The old man hiked up his pants. "Pete O'Brien," he said, holding out a hand.

"Harry Stoner," I said.

Pete O'Brien didn't look like a pornographer—for what that was worth. And if he were, he wasn't a particularly successful one. The warehouse was virtually empty. From the dust on the floors it hadn't seen much business in quite a time. I began to think that the clerk had pulled a fast one.

"You deliver all over the city, Pete?" I asked him.

"Hell, yes. You got some items you want shipped?"

"Not exactly. I'm looking for some goods that you handled."

He looked at me warily. "You an insurance adjustor, Mr. Stoner?"

I shook my head. "I'm a P.I."

"A cop?" Terry said gamely. The grin left his face and was replaced by the sort of amusement that rings like a coin slapped on a bar. It can go either way—heads its violence, tails its back again to explosive laughter.

O'Brien, who'd apparently seen his friend Terry get worked up like that before, looked back over his shoulder and said, "Find something to do, Terry. And I mean now."

The boy got to his feet and took a pull of wine. "The hell," he said quietly. He wiped his lip with a shirt sleeve. "He's a cop, Pete."

O'Brien looked back at me. "Just what is it you want?"

"I'm looking for a girl," I said. I handed him one

of the snapshots I'd picked up at Adult News. "That girl."

"Ho-*lee!*" O'Brien said, looking at the picture.

Terry ambled up and peered over his shoulder. When he saw Cindy Ann, his skin got as red as his hair and his face filled with a coarse lust.

"Shit," he said softly. "Look at that!"

I snapped the picture out of O'Brien's hand. The kid jerked his head up and leered at me. I had enough of leering and of dirty minds for one morning.

"Wipe that smile off your face," I said, before I realized how silly I sounded.

The old man laughed. "Better do like he says, Terry."

"The hell." Terry swaggered a bit—the bottle clutched in his right hand. But I knew it was all for show. I was a lot bigger than he was, and like most bullies, Terry had an instinct for odds. "I don't like you," he said nastily.

"Feel better now that I know?"

The old man laughed again. "Take it over in the corner, Terry. Or this fella's likely to call your bluff."

Terry muttered something under his breath, then took a ferocious pull of the wine. His mouth looked bloody with it when he jerked the bottle away. He walked slowly back to the trolley and plunked himself down and stared at me and drank and muttered to himself.

"Kids," Pete O'Brien said to me. "That one there

hasn't got the guts of a chicken. But he's sure enough vicious when your back is turned."

"I'll keep that in mind."

"You do that," O'Brien said. "About the picture. I don't know where on earth you got the idea that that girl was around here, but I'll tell you plainly she ain't. I've never seen her before in my life. Christ, she sure looks young for that kind of thing."

"She's sixteen," I said. "And I didn't think you'd know her. It's the photograph I'm interested in. It was shipped out of this warehouse."

"Could be," O'Brien said. "We ship all sorts of things. I take it you want to know where that photo came from."

I nodded.

He walked over to a work table next to the door. There was an old ledger on the counter. "I'll tell you the truth, Mr. Stoner. I'm just the floor manager around here. The man you ought to talk to is Morris Rich. He owns this place and he'd be the one that could tell you who ships what from where. That is, if he'd be willing to talk. Which I doubt. Why you looking for that girl?"

"She's a runaway," I said. "Her father wants her back."

O'Brien sighed. "I shouldn't do this, but I'm going to let you look at the manifests. I don't know how much help that'll be. But that's about all I can do for you."

I thanked him and took a quick look at the dusty ledger. There were monthly shipments to the bookstore on Eighth Street, consigned out of Atlanta, where the big pornography houses are based. But the snapshots in my pocket weren't professional smut. They were strictly amateur stuff—the kind of thing that might run as a one-line ad in the back of a magazine. Ten photos for ten dollars and, maybe, a steamy letter to go with them. According to the ledger, there weren't any local shippers dealing with Adult News. Which meant that either the Negro had been lying to me or that he just didn't know where the photos came from. I figured he didn't know. Like Pete O'Brien he was only a hired hand and, as far as he was concerned, everything in the store came from Gem Distributors.

If I was going to go any further, I would have to talk to someone higher up, either to Rich or to whoever owned the porno shop. That is, *if*, as Pete O'Brien said, they were willing to talk to me.

**5**

**IT TURNED OUT** that I didn't have to make that choice, because Pete O'Brien got talkative after I couldn't find anything in the ledger book. Like Hugo Cratz, he was an old man with a heart, and he felt badly enough about Cindy Ann to let drop the fact that Morris Rich not only supplied Adult News, he owned it. Rich had an office in the Dixie Terminal Building on Fifth Street. O'Brien gave me the address as I left, along with a piece of advice.

"Morrie's a family man. The more you say about his kids, the better you make him feel. Just keep talking about his sons and you might make out O.K."

Judging from the decor of Rich's handsome office, I thought O'Brien was probably right. The Rich boys looked down from every wall and up from every end table in the room. And, in case you missed the point, Morrie Rich reminded you by tapping constantly on the dozen picture frames that crowded his desk. I had the disconcerting feeling that his family was sitting there with us. And, eventually, I realized that Rich felt that way, too. Occasionally his nasal voice seemed to soften, and he'd be talking familiarly to one of the boys in the photographs, as if the kid were standing there by his desk, asking his dad for another twenty or for the keys to the Seville.

Morris Rich was a sly, sentimental man of about fifty. A Reds Rooter. A Shriner. A big contributor to the Ruth Lyons' Christmas Fund. A soft touch to his children, who would probably pay for that generosity in later years when someone finally got fed up and told them what selfish, soulless bastards they'd grown up to be. But he was first and foremost a thief. I knew that as soon as I saw him at his huge kidney-shaped desk, sitting behind that photographic phalanx of family and kin. Some men wear their consciences on their sleeves; Morris Rich had his arranged like an army at his feet.

He was a short man with a smooth, hairless head the exact size of a schoolyard kickball and the bright, famished eyes and tiny upturned mouth of a rat. I didn't like him or trust him. And, after a few minutes of listening to him talk about his boys, I realized that he wasn't going to tell me a thing about where the three photographs I'd shown him had come from. Not unless I made finding Cindy Ann a family affair.

"Oh, we ship from all over the world, Mr. Stoner," he said, making a globe with his stubby arms and hugging it to his chest. "It would really be impossible for me to say exactly where *this* item or that item from a lot came from. You see, we're just distributors here at Gem. We don't pack no goods. We don't have no say over what goes into a crate we deliver. Of course, a customer gets mad if what comes out don't tally with what was shipped." He chuckled blandly and dropped his arms to the desk.

"That's too bad," I said. "The girl's family will be very disappointed."

He shook his head sadly. "To be a parent is sometimes a terrible burden. I know. Believe me. Cory, my youngest, is just turning eighteen. I give him a car and he wrecks it. I warn him about girls and he goes out and knocks one up. Cost me eleven hundred dollars to send her to a clinic in New York. And he's still hanging around with her. You explain it."

"I wouldn't know what to say," I said, making my voice cozy and sympathetic. "Hell, I don't know what I'm going to tell the girl's parents as it is. It looks bad when a politician's daughter goes as wrong as this girl has. I don't know what he's going to do. Make a real fuss, I guess."

He bit. Just like I thought he would. His bright, beady eyes danced across the photos and he said, "In the government," in a voice as tight as his little mouth.

It's a shameless business—blackmail. But, like a

football coach, you go with what works. And with Morris Rich what worked was whatever could bring the roof down on his household of boys.

"Ah, it's worse than that," I said. "The guy's got a lot of friends. Listen, if I told you his name you'd understand. He's going to blow a gasket when he learns that I couldn't turn anything up." I shook my head. "What the hell do I care? I did my job. I'll show him the pictures and tell him you just couldn't help me out. I mean business is business, right?"

Morris Rich nodded his head, but his eyes didn't move from my face.

"I hate to take up any more of your time," I said. "But I guess I'd better get a deposition, just in case this thing goes to court. As far as I'm concerned, he'd be better off letting the Feds handle it anyway. They can get court orders, wire taps. You know. Their hands aren't tied. Let them take care of it. Would you mind calling your secretary in for a minute. She can take your statement down. Then we can get it notarized at a bank."

Morris Rich leaned back in his Eames chair and put a finger beside his nose. "You ain't exactly the man you pretend to be, are you, *boy-chik?*"

I threw out my hands. "Hell, Mr. Rich. I'm just a guy trying to make an honest dollar."

"Uh-huh," he said.

Rich held out his hand. "Maybe I should take another look at the photographs."

"Sure," I said politely. "It sometimes pays to take

a second look. Just like with people, sometimes a first impression . . . you don't see clearly."

I handed him the photos and he looked them over quickly.

"What the hell was I thinking of!" he said, slapping his bald head roundly. "I know where these come from. Look, it's"—he glanced at his watch—"almost one-thirty. I'm going to shut down for lunch anyway. What say we go back up to Gem and take a look at the manifests, just to be sure?"

"I already saw the manifests, Mr. Rich."

He got a pained look in his eyes. "You ain't supposed to look at those books, Mr. Stoner. I don't know what Pete was thinking of to show them to you."

"Well, I guess he just got carried away by the pictures."

"Uh-huh." Rich tapped nervously at the picture frames on his desk and I dragged one foot across the floor and made swirls in the plush carpet. And that's the way we would have remained—me making swirls and Rich playing those picture frames like a brassy xylophone—if I hadn't gotten to my feet with a mild groan and told him what he would never know was the absolute truth.

"I'm getting tired of this game, Mr. Rich. If you've got some information about the whereabouts of this girl, it would be in your best interest to tell me now, before this thing gets out of hand."

"Are you threatening me?" he said with alarm.

"I got lawyers who can handle this, if you're threatening me."

"We both know it would be cleaner to keep this thing out of court, Mr. Rich. You don't want cops crawling around your warehouse and your bookstore, do you?"

"What bookstore?" he said. "I don't know nothing about no bookstore."

I looked at him ruefully. "All right, Mr. Rich. I guess you know better than I do how much heat you can take."

I was almost to the door, past those walls of smiling Rich boys, when he called me back.

# 6

THE WHITE FRAME house was on River Road, along the stretch of bottomland that is flooded yearly when the Ohio crests in the spring. I could smell the rot from where I'd parked the car on a clay embankment—that fecal smell of decay that troubles the river where it goes shallow and dead. It made me think of the war and of the jungle heat and of the bodies that puffed up like drowned men in the steamy rain forests.

A beat-up white Falcon was parked next to the house, and there was an old tire lying on its side in the grassless front yard. It looked a likely enough spot for a pornographer to hole up, although an hour before Morris Rich had tried to convince me that the man who was holed up there would be better off left alone.

"Jones is his name. Abel Jones," he said to me.

"But, believe me, it should have been the other one —Cain. He's a very tough customer, Mr. Stoner. I get snapshots from him once and a while. Polaroids. He's the only one who sells me Polaroids. That's why I know the ones you showed me are from him. I bought 'em maybe a month ago. Always they're different girls. And sometimes I can't even display them."

Rich laughed hollowly. "He ain't a family man, Mr. Stoner. Not like me. He likes to hurt. I'd advise you to stay away from him."

Morris Rich didn't want any trouble, from the police or the F.B.I. or anyone who might bring a curse on his house and business. But he'd made me think twice before I got out of the Pinto and hiked down to that lone frame house. In the flats, the nearest help was a good two hundred yards to the east, which meant that anything short of a canon blast would die away in the hot, fetid wind coming off the river. It really did smell like jungle warfare in the yard, although the only tree in sight was a dead elm painted white on the trunk.

I tried to shake the bad memories out of my head as I walked up to the porch. There was no bell by the screen door, so I rattled the frame with my fist. A few seconds later, a young woman dressed in a long red shift padded up.

"Are you from the gas?" she said belligerently.

She had long black hair braided in a ponytail, black eyes of the dull, opalescent sheen of oil paintings, and a round, Indian face that would have been pretty if it weren't for a yellow birthmark that ran down her left cheek like Ahab's ivory scar.

I told her I wasn't from the gas.

"Well, somebody better come out," she said wearily. " 'Cause we paid the damn bill over a week ago."

She made a little smile of excuse, while her eyes worked me over. "You're a cop, aren't you?" she said.

Some people have that gift. But they've usually paid a price for it. This one looked too young to have paid in full. So I guessed that cops and gasmen were no strangers to the house.

"I'm a P.I.," I told her. "I'm looking for Abel Jones."

"He's not here."

"Then I'll wait."

She shook her head slightly, as if what I'd said had amused her. "No, you won't. He won't want to see you."

"How can you be sure?"

"Because *I* don't want to see you," she said flatly. "Now, beat it!"

She started to walk away from the door when a man's husky voice called to her from upstairs. "Who is it?"

She gave me a quick amused look over her shoulder—half-warning, half-reproach. It made me like her a little, though I'd be damned if I knew why.

Abel Jones came trundling down the stairs. I got

him a little at a time. First his bare toes. Then three feet of black gabardine slacks. Then three more feet of thin pink belly and hairless chest. Then his face, shaded with a day's growth of beard. He looked to be around forty, and he had the sharp mean features of the Appalachian tough—narrow lips, a nose that could open an envelope, black eyes, and gaunt, grooved cheeks.

He passed a hand through his dark, unkempt hair and said, "What is it? What do you want?" in a drunken, hostile voice.

"I'd like to talk to you, Mr. Jones."

He laughed a little when I said "mister."

"You would?" he said. "What about?"

"This porch is no place to talk."

"It's my house!" he shouted, as if I were about to put a torch to it. "Don't dare talk down my home!"

He looked me over, the way the girl had. "Well, come in, then."

He pushed at the screen door and I walked through.

"You dicks is all alike," he said. "Think you can come in and run down a man's home."

I followed him through an archway into a living room that could have been decorated by Hugo Cratz. All plaid and plastic and faded stripe, dotted like a prize booth at a county fair with stuffed animals and plastic trophies. The same stale smells hung in the air, mixed with a tang of whiskey and tobacco.

Jones sat down on a torn vinyl recliner. "Get us

something to drink, Coral," he said to the girl. He said it with relish, as if he were hoping I'd turn him down.

Coral winked at me and sauntered out of the room. She was naked under that shift and she moved with a studied sensuality.

"I understand you sell pictures," I said, sitting across from him on a hard, red plastic chair.

"Who told you that?"

"That isn't important."

I took one of the photographs of Cindy Ann out of my pocket and tossed it over to him.

Jones slapped the snapshot facedown on his knee. Then he flicked its edge and peeked at it the way a man peeks at a hole-card. It occurred to me that he wouldn't have to squeeze out that look if there wasn't a good chance that he wasn't going to like what he saw.

"So what?" he said, pitching the photo back to me.

"I want the girl," I said to him.

"Well, you can want what you want, mister. But you ain't going to get nothing out of me."

Coral came back into the room with a bottle of Old Grandad and three glasses in her right hand.

She poured three drinks and handed one to me and one to Jones.

"Cheers," she said, raising her own glass.

Jones tossed down the bourbon. He hadn't taken his vicious little eyes off me since I'd showed him the snapshot. But that didn't mean much. A man like

Jones only has one expression and, like a kid on Christmas day, he likes to set it up and see it work. I concentrated on the girl and tried to read his mood in her face. If my reading was correct, I was in for some trouble, because Coral's dark eyes touched on everything in the room but me. It was as if she were calculating just how much damage she'd have to repair when Abel got through. From the disgust on her face, she saw a lot of work ahead.

"You ain't touched your drink, *mister*," Jones said.

Coral let out a sigh. "There doesn't have to be any trouble, does there?"

"Shut up!" Jones said.

"No, Abel. I'm not going to shut up. This is my house, and I'm not going to see it busted up again. Let me see that photograph."

Jones stood up and walked over to where Coral was standing in the archway next to the front hall. "Get the hell out of here," he said to her. "Or there will be trouble."

That was my cue. I stood up. "No, there won't, Abel."

He whirled around to face me.

He balled his fists and started toward me when Coral shrieked. And I mean shrieked—a real movie-land scream that made the room ring and stopped Abel Jones in his tracks.

He lowered his fists and turned back to where Coral was standing. "Now just why the hell'd you do that, Coral?" he said in a cranky voice that was probably as close to amusement as Abel Jones ever got. "You 'bout scared the shit out of me."

"Good," she said.

He shook his head forlornly and looked back at me.

"Takes most of the fun out of it, doesn't it?" I said.

Jones shook his head again, walked back over to the recliner, and plopped down.

"That's the first sane thing you've done in a month," Coral said to him. "Now, show me that picture."

I dug it out of my coat pocket. She studied it dispassionately for a moment.

"Before I say anything," she said. "I want to be clear. That mean son-of-a-bitch over there would just as soon kill you as look at you. And don't think he couldn't, mister." She tossed her handsome head at Abel. "You're big all right. But he's as merciless as a New Mexican rattlesnake. And I don't want to see this place get torn up again."

"I'm not the law," I told her. "I'm a private cop. And your boy can pander as many dirty pictures as he likes, once I find that girl."

"What's so important about this little slut?" She tapped the photograph.

"Her father wants her back."

Coral glanced at Jones, who was still sitting stock still in the chair, contemplating a world of freakish folly.

"He's no pornographer," she said with a touch

of contempt in her voice. "He does favors for the people who gave him those photographs. He's supposed to get rid of them, but Abel there just can't stand to see an easy buck slide by. So every now and then he sells a bundle to Morrie Rich."

She nudged my arm with her elbow. "Look at him there. Just meditating like a Krishna what he's going to do to me once you leave." She laughed grimly. "You're going to cost me a black eye, mister. Doesn't that make you feel good?"

I started to volunteer some help, but Coral gave me a quick furious look, full of family pride and short temper.

"Don't," she said simply. "Not if you want to get out of here in one piece. Just leave it alone. I don't know about that girl. Neither does he, even though he'd die and take you and me with him before he told you that. But the people he gets those pictures from do a lot of business over in Newport. You might try over there."

"What kind of business do they do?"

Coral shook her head. "I've said enough. Now why don't you just get the hell out of here before he comes out of that trance and kills you."

———

I was halfway across the desolate front yard when I heard someone coming up behind me. It gave me a start, the way Coral's scream had startled me. I'd already drawn my pistol before I realized it was the girl and not Abel Jones. She glanced scornfully at the gun in my hand.

"You and Abel aren't as different as I thought," she said.

I tucked the gun in my pocket. "Yes, we are," I said.

She didn't believe me. And, for a brief second, I wanted to tell her why she was wrong.

I liked Coral. She was tough, handsome, and honest, and she deserved better than the likes of Abel Jones. The sad part was that the Abel Joneses of this world were precisely the ones she would always end up with. She'd always be that wrong about her men, always mistake petty cowardice for a tender heart and cruelty for strength. And she'd always be too damn hopeful to undo the mistake.

I wanted to tell her that, but I didn't.

"I only came out here to get away from him," she said, brushing a strand of black hair from her face. "He'll go upstairs in awhile and fall asleep again. And if I'm lucky, he won't remember much of it when he wakes up."

She shaded her eyes and stared up at the embankment, where the steep green hills came down on the west side of River Road. The sun was dropping behind them, now, and behind us, the river was all golden to the Kentucky shore. "Must be close to five," she said and looked shyly toward me.

"What is it, Coral?" I said. "What do you want to tell me?"

"I'm going to be leaving here soon," she said.

"Just pick up and go. Let the house, if anybody'll have it." She looked back at the porch. "That's my inheritance. That's all I got left, holding me here."

"Maybe Jones'll come with you," I said.

She smiled sadly. "No. I don't think so. But it's good of you to say it. He'll stay on, probably. He wouldn't know what to do without his liquor and his friends." Coral took a deep breath. "I guess what I came out here to do was to say all of that to you. It's kind of like saying goodbye, without saying it face to face."

I nodded. "Glad I could help."

She straightened up and pulled at her shift where it had bunched at her waist. Then her dark face turned red, and she looked down at the marl. I had the feeling that, having said goodbye to Abel, she'd suddenly remembered that she was an attractive woman and that I was a man. And it had embarrassed her, as if she'd done something wicked behind Jones's back.

"He really doesn't know about that girl," she said, changing the subject. "They never tell him the names."

"Why do they need to get rid of the pictures at all?"

"I couldn't say. He just gets 'em. And sometimes he throws them out and sometimes he sells them."

"What kind of business do they run?"

"A rough one. I guess I can tell you that much. It sure doesn't pay to be on the wrong side of that girl."

"Laurie Jellicoe?" I said.

Her eyes darted to my face. "If you knew that name, why'd you come here?"

"Because that name is all I know. All I'm trying to do is find out what they're doing with the girl. Whether it's pornography or something more."

"Look, mister," she said and her face grew somber. "Why don't you tell whoever it is that's looking for this girl to forget her? You'll save yourself a lot of trouble. They don't give things up easy, those two. I know. I've seen how they work. People they don't like, people that get in their way, just don't last very long. That girl who went off with them knew what she was doing. Why not just leave it at that?"

"It's not up to me," I said.

"Well, then, keep that kid's old man out of harm's way," she said sternly. "Or both you and he will regret it. Get out of here, now. Before he comes out and starts a ruckus."

"Good luck," I said to her.

I started up the clay embankment and looked back once when I got to the car. But she'd already gone in.

She was right about one thing. From the looks of Abel Jones, a meddlesome old man like Hugo *would* be better off out of the way. Better for him, better for me, and, maybe, better for Cindy Ann.

# 7

**WE WENT OUT** to dinner that night, Hugo Cratz and I. We drove down Cornell to Ludlow and three blocks south to the nondescript gray and white cube of the Busy Bee.

He'd cleaned himself up for the meal. Put on a fresh checked shirt and a red cardigan sweater and scraped at the stubble on his chin. And, as we walked from the parking lot to the street, I caught a bit of bounce, a bit of military cadence, in his step. He was enjoying it, what he thought was the honor of it, which was fine with me. A little back-slapping and a few beers and we both might find the nerve to strike a compromise.

The restaurant was crowded, so I took Hugo up to the big dark U-shaped bar on the second level—an elevated terrace about six steps above the ground floor—and introduced him to Hank Greenberg, the barkeep.

We ordered two beers and, after taking a quick look at Hugo, I decided it would be better if we both sat down to talk. "We'll be over in the corner," I called to Hank and pointed to an empty booth to the left of the bar.

"Right," he said.

We were almost there. We'd almost made it—Hugo tottering a little as we maneuvered through the crowd, me pushing gently at his back—when a big square sallow-faced man, with the name "Mike" tagged on his shirtfront and a blue Navy anchor tattooed on his left forearm, inadvertently clobbered the old man and sent him tumbling back into me. I caught Hugo by the arms and pulled him to his feet. Big Mike dropped drunkenly into our booth and, with a sigh of unexpected pleasure, started drinking the beers that Hank had just deposited on the table.

"Hey!" I shouted over the top of Hugo's wispy head. "Those are our beers."

"He's drunk, mister," a gaunt man with the name "Al" on his shirt said from the bar rail. "Don't mess with him. He's just plain red-eyed mean when he's stiff like that."

"Those are our beers," I said to him.

Al shrugged. "It's your funeral."

Hugo was wobbling a bit, so I turned him around and looked him over. A little blood was oozing from his nose.

"It ain't nothing. That moose just clipped me is

all, with his elbow. Say, mister?" he said to Mike. "You ought to watch where you're going."

Mike looked up balefully, the way a big, bad-tempered shepherd dog looks up from his food bowl. "Go to hell," he growled.

The moralist in me was getting a good work-out that day. But I managed to check him. He had bigger fish to fry than a barroom loudmouth.

"C'mon Hugo," I said. "Let's get you cleaned up."

Hugo washed himself off in the john, and as we walked back down to the restaurant level, Big Mike raised a glass to us. "Goddamn pissant," Hugo hissed. And gave me a withering look.

Jo Riley, the hostess at the Busy Bee, seated us at a relatively quiet table in a corner of the main room.

On duty Jo wears pale pink lipstick, piles her coal-black hair in a massive bee-hive, and carries a pair of sequined glasses on a silver-metal chain around her neck. She fancies long, high-necked, colorless dresses for the same reason she wears her hair unfashionably and sports those bridge club spectacles. In a job like hers, in a place like the Busy Bee, the last thing Jo needs is a table full of rowdies making passes at her. And, believe me, with her hair down, her skirt shortened, and those glasses in the case where they belong, Jo is something to become rowdy about. I'd gotten pretty rowdy myself about three years before, and there was still something volatile between us. We'd been lucky. We'd shared some good times and we'd parted. And there'd been no big scene at the end. No blow-up to color what had come before, to make the pleasure seem illusory. We'd just drifted apart, each to another partner and another bed. Both of us had sense enough not to tempt fate by giving it a second try; both of us, I think, knew that if it didn't work this time, there *would* be that blow-up; and neither of us wanted to forfeit that legacy of past perfect. So we generally smiled at each other, blushed, and chatted nonsense, while memory whispered in another language beneath our patter.

"This is Hugo Cratz," I said to Jo. "A client."

"Really?" she said, raising a friendly eyebrow. She was perfect, Jo. So good at her job she was breathtaking. The eyebrow had been just right. Not coy, not condescending. Just warm and deferential like a tip of a hat. "What can I get you?" she said sweetly to Hugo.

It worked. He hemmed and hawed and smiled and blushed and finally said, "Beer?" like he was asking his pretty fourth-grade teacher if she were already married.

"I thought so," Jo said approvingly. "Two Buds, then, Harry?"

I nodded and smiled at her. Some Jo.

We ordered the shrimp salads with the Bee's tangy, horseradishy dressing, and when Jo walked off to the bar, Hugo said to me: "Nice girl. You two friends?"

"You don't miss much, do you, Hugo?"

"Nope," he chuckled. "Like seeing how there

was no reason we couldn't talk back at my place, I figure you brought me here to tell me something you wasn't prepared to say on my home turf."

I shook my head. "Drink your beer, will you, Hugo?"

"O.K., Harry," Hugo Cratz said.

We drank and ate and between Hugo's Marine stories and my M.P. stories, we generally had a pretty good time. After supper, the Bee started to empty and Jo pulled up a chair and shared a beer with us at our table. I'd like to think that Hugo Cratz had an especially good time that evening. I'd like to think that between Jo and the beer and me he stopped thinking about his Cindy Ann—at least for awhile—and about the death that haunted his cramped apartment. He looked good, for what that's worth. Animated, ruddy. And he talked— talked for hours in a cheerful, spirited voice—about the past.

Around eleven o'clock, while Jo tended the ta- bles and the pianist tickled out a jaunty rendition of "St. Louis Blues," Hugo leaned across the table and said, "I guess it's time."

I knew what he meant.

"One thing, though," he said. "I want you to know, whatever it is you got to say, I've had a real fine evening. And I thank you for it."

"I've had a fine evening too, Hugo."

His thin mouth trembled a bit and he sighed.

"If you want her back Hugo . . ." I didn't know quite how to say it, or maybe I just couldn't bring myself to hurt him that way. "If you want to maximize the possibilities . . . you're going to have to do what I say."

"What're you building up to, Harry?"

"Let's say the Jellicoes have hidden Cindy Ann away somewhere. Maybe they've got her making movies. Maybe they're hiring her out. I don't know exactly what the set-up is yet. That's the first thing I've got to find out."

"How you going to do that?" Hugo said.

"I found out today that the Jellicoes may have her working in Newport. I've got some friends on that side of the river," I told him. "One man, in particular, who knows just about every shady character in Kentucky. If the Jellicoes are running any kind of independent porno game or if they've got a stable of girls for sale, this friend will know about it."

"All right," Hugo said. "I take it he ain't a friend in the strict sense of the word?"

I laughed. "No. Just a contact I picked up over the years. Working with the D.A. and Pinkerton and so on."

"All right. What next?"

"They've got Cindy Ann. That gives them the hole card as far as *we're* concerned."

"The whole deck," Hugo said glumly.

I shook my head. "Uh-uh. We've got the shoe box. That's the joker. From what I learned today, the Jellicoes don't want photographs like the ones you've got in circulation. Don't ask me why, because I don't know that yet. But, if I can convince them that those pictures of yours are valuable, maybe I can work a trade—what I know and what you know for Cindy Ann."

Hugo sipped meditatively at his beer. "When I was in the Corps they used to run us through a little exercise 'bout once every other day. They'd station a machine gun up on a little rise. And this gun would spray live ammo across a field. And in this field there'd be rocks and logs and mud and standing water. And what we was supposed to do was crawl across it whilst this machine gun was firing over our fannies. It took a real nice sense of judgment to know when to lift up and when to duck down. Too high and you'd get your britches blown off. Too low and you'd just get stuck there whilst the rest of your buddies crawled on by. Strikes me that what you're proposing is a little like that exercise. You aim to convince the Jellicoes that those photographs are valuable. Strikes me that value can mean different things to different folks. You make 'em seem too valuable and that tree of Laurie's is likely to topple over on you. You make 'em seem not valuable enough and they're just likely to brush you off like a fly."

I smiled at him. "You should've been a detective, Hugo."

"I'd have been a good one."

"Yep."

"So where do I fit into this scheme of yours?"

I took a swallow of beer and said, "You don't."

At first, he didn't say anything at all. Just stared

off into space—cogitating, digesting it. After a second he turned in the booth seat and looked me in the eye. "I want you to tell me the truth. If you want me out of the way 'cause I'd just be in it every other second, that's one thing. If you're trying to get rid of me 'cause you're worried about something happening to me, that's another. Now, which is it?"

"I work alone, Hugo. That's what I get paid for. I'm not saying that you're less of a man than I am or that you can't take care of yourself. But, with the stakes so high, I do it my way or I don't do it at all. And my way means you clear out. You go off to Dayton and visit your son."

"For how long?"

"Until I *need* you to come back."

Hugo took a deep breath. "All right, Harry. I'll leave tomorrow."

"Good," I said. "And no tricks, Hugo."

"Why, Harry!" he said. "Whatever made you say a thing like that?"

We had another round of beers. Hugo seemed too damn cheerful, and I began to wonder just how seriously he'd taken my point. Around twelve, he said, "I been out too late." So I stood up and took the check up to the bar. I was standing next to the cash register when someone shoved me so hard that I knocked over a couple of beer glasses.

I turned around and saw the back of Big Mike's head. He was a fair-sized gent, Big Mike. My height, but a good fifty pounds heavier than I was and at least a fifth drunker. Maybe it was Terry and Morris

Rich; maybe it was Abel Jones and the Jellicoes; maybe it was Cindy Ann; or maybe it was the beer and the talk and the sneaking suspicion that Hugo hadn't heard a word that I'd said. But that angry little man inside of me had had his fill of nastiness for one day. "I'm taking over," he said. And I was just too tired and dejected to say, "No."

I tapped Mike on the shoulder and he turned slowly around. He was in his cups, all right. But he was one of those mean, deceptive drunks. His square, porcine face was flushed and sweaty; but the liquor hadn't gotten into his eyes yet. And those eyes were just aching for trouble.

"Hey, Mike!" I said, clapping him on the arm. "You run down any more old men tonight?"

"What're you talking about?" he said in a loud, gravelly voice.

"Hell, I'm talking about that two bucks you owe me for those two beers of mine you drank."

Mike's bloodshot eyes narrowed. "I remember you. You're the boy that was sucking around with that old faggot."

"That's it," I said cheerfully. "Now how about my two bucks?"

"Go to hell," Big Mike said.

"Give the man the two bucks, will you, mister?" Hank said from behind the register. "You took the beer. I saw you do it."

"And who the hell are you?" Mike roared. "You can't even have a drink in this faggot bar without some fairy sucking up to you."

"Don't call me that," Hank said.

That was it. That was all big Mike had been waiting for. He froze like a guard dog before he pounces and stared with dull hatred at Hank. "What did you say to me, faggot?"

"He said not to call him that," I said.

Big Mike whirled with impossible quickness and threw a deft right hand at my head. At the time you never know how something so swift and violent can miss its mark. Either you move or you fall—it's that simple. I moved, ducking in under Mike's right shoulder. He was a little off balance, but he'd be squared around in a second. And I wasn't going to wait. I threw a hard right jab and caught him full in the solar plexis.

"Oh," Mike groaned and fell backward onto the floor.

As I started in after him, Hank slapped his arm across my chest.

"Easy, Harry," he said. "He's had enough."

"I want my two bucks," I said between my teeth.

"Here," one of Mike's friends said. "Here, I'll give you the two bucks."

"I want it from *him!*" I said, kicking Big Mike hard in the ass.

"Harry," Hank said.

Big Mike groaned.

"I'll get it for you," the one called Al said. He bent over Mike and pulled his wallet from his trousers. "Here," he said, tossing it to me.

I pulled two singles from the billfold and threw the wallet on the floor.

"Don't you *ever* bring that asshole in here again," I said to Al. "You hear?"

"Goodnight, Harry," Jo cooed.

I walked down to the restaurant level, plucked Hugo by the arm, and walked quickly into the warm night air.

"Boy," he said to me, as we turned for the parking lot. "Looks like I picked me the right man."

# 8

**MORNINGS AFTER ARE** generally a bad time for me. Either the blood sugars are too low or my heart isn't pounding energetically enough or the dreamy rhythms of night are still playing in my ears. For half an hour after I've opened my eyes, I blunder through the apartment like a sleep-walker and try to fend off that first uncensored rush of memories. But the dead faces, the maimed ones, the friends whom violence has borne away, always crowd in. And that Saturday morning was no different. Tough black Roscoe Bohannon—dead three years—and beautiful Lauren Swift—dead one—an enemy and a friend, were there when I opened my eyes. Night travelers, lost in the daylight, they drifted like motes in the clear noon sun and wouldn't be chased away until I'd lifted myself from bed and plunged into a shower.

Then the routines began. The morning coffee on the living room couch. The sound of the Zenith Globemaster, which I play constantly so that I'll always be in earshot of a human voice. The waxy feel and inky smell of newsprint. My half-hour passed, and I found that I could make a sentence, the first of the day: *Get in touch with Hugo Cratz.*

I walked over to the phone on the rolltop desk beneath the living room window and dialed Hugo's home. The previous night filtered back to me as I listened to it ring. The turquoise blue discoloration of the first knuckle of my middle finger reminded me of the fight with Mike. And then I remembered the pleasure in Hugo's voice as we'd walked out to the car. He'd been too pleased, too self-satisfied, too nonchalant. He was up to something, I was sure of it. Formulating some scheme that would keep him from leaving town. At first, it might delay him for an afternoon. Then a day. Then a week. And, before I knew it, old Hugo would have manipulated me into letting him stay on—to bully and cheer me as I jousted with Lance and Laurie for the honor of Cindy Ann.

That wasn't going to happen. If I had to put him on the bus myself and watch it leave and call like a worried mother when he arrived, that wasn't going to happen. The truth was I liked the old codger too much to see him hurt. And, if Coral was right, that's what could happen.

He answered the phone on the twentieth ring, in that high-pitched, hurky-jerky voice and, when I reminded him that he was leaving that day, he said: "Yes. All right, Harry. Whatever you think is best."

I half expected to find him gone when I pulled into his driveway at half-past one that afternoon. But there he was, sitting on the porch chair, shading his eyes with one hand and gripping a straw valise in the other. I honked and Hugo walked down the front steps, cracked open the car door, and slid onto the seat.

"What kept you?" he said cheerfully.

I gave him a sidelong look. His chin was bristling again with salt-and-pepper stubble; and his nose took little swipes at it when he worked his jaws, which he did with mechanical regularity, as if he were chewing a wad of tobacco or talking to himself. And those wet blue eyes, like eyes in a clear aspic, were nervous and merry.

"Just what are you so cheerful about?" I asked him, throwing the Pinto into reverse and backing out onto Cornell. "Did you call your son?"

"Yep." He nodded. "Called him this morning. He's been trying to get me to come up there for years. Said he'd build a room addition for me if I promised to stay for good."

"Uh-huh," I said, guiding us onto Ludlow and west to the expressway. "You call the bus station like I told you to?"

"Sure did," Hugo said. "She leaves at two-fifteen and arrives in Dayton at four-thirty. Ralph'll be at the depot to pick me up."

"Uh-huh," I said. "Did you remember to bring the key to your place and the shoebox?"

"Got 'em in my bag, Harry. Just like you told me."

I bit my lip.

"You sure are nervous, Harry," Hugo said placidly.

"I just don't want to forget anything, Hugo," I said, turning onto I-75 and heading south out of the Clifton hillside along the sunny industrial flats on the outskirts of town. "I don't want to give you any reason to show up on my doorstep tomorrow."

"Aw, Harry," he said.

At two sharp we pulled up beneath the prancing neon greyhound above the bus terminal entrance. I slipped a quarter into the meter and Hugo moseyed toward the depot.

"Wait up!" I barked at him.

He stopped dead at the door and pretended to read the schedules and travel posters in the display cases.

"You sure are nervous," Hugo said again, as we walked out of the keen white sunlight and into the shade of the terminal.

No matter how noisy a bus terminal gets—and on a July Saturday they get pretty damn loud—you can always hear your own footsteps echoing above the crackle of the loudspeakers, the hiss of air brakes, the soft sigh of bus doors opening, and the amplified roar of the diesels as they pull out of their loading docks. I don't know how they do it, how they calculate the eigentones and reflecting angles to bring the click of heels and shoe leather into such crisp prominence. Nor do I understand why bus stations are always made to look so dreary. Or why the people sitting on the hard blue-and-red plastic benches are invariably as cheerless and sullen-looking as the gaunt men and women in Walker Evans's studies of the rural poor. Even the attendants and guards are seedy and impassive; and everyone looks too damn bored to talk about it. If there's an urban hell, the bus station must come pretty close to being it.

I shadowed Hugo as he picked up his ticket and, together, we walked down to the basement lockers. Hugo got the shoebox out of his valise; and, after taking three of the photographs out and slipping them into my pocket, I shoved the box into a fifty-cent cubicle and locked it shut.

"O.K., Hugo," I said. "Let's go."

The old man pivoted lightly on one foot and said, "You don't have to stick around, Harry. I can find my way to the bus."

I smiled and shook my head ruefully. I'd known it was coming; I just hadn't known what form it was going to take. Actually I was a little disappointed that Hugo had thought he could get rid of me so easily.

"Now just a second," he said, as I tugged him by the coat sleeve. "Just a minute, here."

"It isn't going to work, Hugo," I said.

"I ain't no damn kid," he said testily, "that has to be watched over every second."

I grabbed his arm firmly and picked up the straw suitcase. "Let's go."

"Now, Harry."

I walked him to the loading area and he cursed and muttered and fumed every step of the way. "You can't do this to me. This is a free country. . . . I got my rights. . . . Damn it, Harry, let go of my arm . . . the way they treat old folks in this city is a crime. . . ."

When he saw that it wasn't going to work, Hugo grew sly and pensive looking. "I didn't call my damn son," he said suddenly. "There ain't going to be nobody there to meet me."

"That's tough, Hugo. You'll just have to walk a few blocks."

"I'm recovering from a stroke," he whined. "You ain't going to put me out in the hot sun and make me walk till I keel over, are you?"

"Yeah." I nodded. "That's what I'm going to do."

"You ain't got a drop of pity in you, Harry," Hugo said bitterly. "If I drop dead on the streets of Dayton, my blood'll be on your head. Are you willing to live with that guilt?"

"You'll be all right, Hugo," I said with a sigh. "I called your son myself this morning. And he'll be there to meet you."

"You called Ralph?" Hugo said in a little voice.

I nodded. "This morning, Hugo."

He shrivelled like a spent balloon. "Damn," he said, shaking his wispy white head.

Hugo didn't say another word until the bus arrived. As the passengers queued up beside the door, he got slowly to his feet. "You'll be careful, now, won't you, Harry?" he said in a forlorn voice. "You won't let nothing bad happen, now, will you?"

"No," I said, smiling at him. "Nothing bad will happen."

"And you'll call me once and awhile, won't you? To let me know how things are?"

"Sure I will."

"About the money," he said, rubbing his grizzled chin.

"We'll talk about that when I've got Cindy Ann back for you."

Hugo patted his coat pockets and his pants pockets and sighed. "Well," he said, holding out his hand. "Looks like I got everything."

I shook his hand and said, "The key."

"Huh?" Hugo looked at me uncertainly.

"The key to your apartment, Hugo. I want it."

Hugo blew a little air out of his mouth and cursed violently. "You don't miss much either," he said, clawing at his pants pocket. "Do you, Mister Harry Stoner?"

"I try not to."

"Well, just you keep it up," he said as he walked up to the bus door. "You hear?" Hugo stepped up onto the bus. "And try to make this quick, will you?" he called out as the bus door sighed shut. "A few weeks with Ralph and I'll be ready for the V.A. hospital."

# 9

ONCE I'D SEEN Hugo safely off, I walked up Fifth Street to a pancake house at the corner of Elm and contemplated the world over a plate of doughy waffles. From where I was sitting Elm seemed to be full of girls in bright summer dresses, and each one of them looked as if she had just stepped off the bus from Greenburg or Sunman or Milan. Perhaps from as far away as Sioux Falls, wherever the hell that was. Each of them had the same look on her face—that dreamy, vacant look that comes when the eye is turned inward and fully in love with what it sees. It was like an erotic daydream out there on the blazing street, a predator's dream of ripe and easy pickings, a world of Cindy Anns. I took a sip of bitter coffee and, when I looked up again, the girls seemed to have grown a lot wiser.

It's not you, ladies, I said to myself. It's just me.

Just me and a handful of photographs that I can't get out of my mind. I pressed my coat pocket and felt the little square that the snapshots made under the fabric. When this was just a market town, maybe Cindy Ann could have afforded to come here wide-eyed and unwary. But cities grow up like psychopathic children. They grow up and become delinquents. Even cities as strict and unglamorous as this one. Years pass and what is just a smirk or a piece of conventional wisdom out in the farmlands becomes an industry in the flats.

I paid my check at the register and walked down Fifth to the bus terminal. The meter was just running out as I got to the car. But that was all right. I had a trip to make anyway. I had a captain of industry to see.

═══

From the Ohio side, Newport, Kentucky, seems a small, colorful hamlet nestled in green hills. On the river bank the posh marinas reach baby-white fingers out into the clear run of the Ohio. Speedboats chase up and down the shore, towing an occasional skier in their wakes. Above the water's edge Newport rises in a talus of shale and seems to keep rising gently in a sweep of white and red roofs that have the sleepy look of adobe and sunbaked tile. And everywhere that isn't white or red is green with the maple trees that cascade down from the surrounding hillsides and flood through the hamlet in a wave that stops just short of the river bank. From the

Ohio shore, Newport has the look of one of those vacation communities that people like Cox and Meyer plant on the edges of newly dredged lakes and call Sunwood or Lake of the Four Pines. From the Kentucky side, it's a different view entirely.

For one thing, you're suddenly aware that there is a big city behind you—a clean expanse of bright glass and structured steel and china-red brick. The little one and two-story businesses that dot the main drags of Newport seem very small indeed, by comparison. And the age that shows on them is anything but picturesque. Once you've settled down in the garden streets that criss-cross the town proper, the summery look of vacation quickly fades. The houses are frame and the paint is peeling everywhere and the streets are littered with broken glass and in need of patching. And the men and women who live on the streets have the unmistakable look of the urban poor—so pinched and chalk-white in the face and on the arms and legs that you would think, in Newport, that a suntan was something you had to be able to afford.

The "poor cousin" look of Newport is deceptive. There *is* money in the city, but it's concentrated and virtually hidden away in the auto dealerships that proliferate like cement ponds along the riverfront and in the night clubs that seem to occupy whole blocks of the business district. It doesn't take a trained eye to discover where most of the dollars have gone. Not when the City Hall is an old brick firehouse and the Pink Kittycat Club looks like a small Vegas hotel. The men who work that stretch of town never lack a tan, even in the dead of winter. And the clothes they wear have creases in them that could cut bread.

Every city has a reason for being where it is. And Newport's reason is to service Cincinnati, to provide the gambling, the prostitution, and the sin that the good elders of our town have turned out of the city limits. Newport is an open secret, a dirty little joke that nobody laughs at because there's too much muscle and money in Newport to make it a fun or a funny place. It's a tough, leering border town, with a wide-open police department and a come-hither night life. And every one of those good Cincinnati burghers is very glad it's around. There has to be some place for the convention trade to go. There has to be some place for the businessmen from Elkhart and Louisville and Dayton to blow off a little steam. And Newport is the place. Let the conventioneer dine in Cincinnati, put up in a good Cincinnati hotel. Let him cheer the Reds in the early evening and grab a drink or two downtown. And, then, let him cross the river, with the city's blessing, and find some harder action. Most of the money ends up in Cincinnati's pocket, anyway. Most of it is Cincinnati money to begin with.

There are two or three people in Newport who are above what little law there is. And one of them is "Porky" Simlab, the man I was going to see. There is a story about Porky that bears repeating. It took place thirty years ago, when Newport was even more of a wide open town than it is today. At the time, Porky and his wife Blanche owned the Golden Deer on Main—a bar and strip joint that had a raucous and highly profitable second floor. It's said that two out-of-towners, independents with loose gangland credentials, moved in on Porky's gold mine, first by trying to buy him out and then by trying to drive him out. There were words and, one afternoon, Blanche Simlab got into her pink Cadillac and came back out through the windshield, in a fiery blast that tore the car and Blanche in two. The next day, Porky sold the Golden Deer to the two men from out of town and went into a different line of work. He bought a motion picture theater on the north side of the city, became a model citizen, and, two or three years later, ran for mayor on a reform ticket. He was elected by a landslide. Everyone loved good ol' Porky, who was and is a tubby country boy with a fat placid face and an odd habit of winking with his mouth instead of with his little brown eyes. Once Porky got into office, in that shed they call "City Hall," he made a counter-proposal to the two businessmen from out of town who had purchased the Golden Deer. It wasn't a question of the price being wrong—no money was offered. It was more of a case of escheat, of property returning to its rightful owner, with a provision that the new owners leave town. Of course, the two owners didn't think much of the deal. So, one cold February night in 1952, Porky authorized a raid on the Golden Deer and insisted that his police hot-load their revolvers and shotguns, in case of trouble. There wasn't much trouble. The cops came through the door about one hour after closing and killed every man and woman on the first floor of the night club. And a week later Porky Simlab repossessed the Golden Deer.

He never did let go of the motion picture theater and, about ten years after the night of the Golden Deer raid, he bought another one—a first-run house in Erlanger that specializes in Disney films, wholesome family entertainment. By then, Porky was legend in Boone County. A local character who drove around in a pink El Dorado with bull's horns for a hood ornament and who held daily court on the slat porch of his modest home on Charles Street, with his feet up on the railing, his rear parked in a bentwood rocker, and his mouth winking away in that fat baby face with its unsmiling eyes. He was a soft-spoken, cracker-jack country hood, who dressed in tieless white linen shirts with flat splayed collars and two-piece leisure suits of a loamy brown. I'd first met him in 1968 when I was working for Pinkerton and he'd taken a "shine" to me. He'd invited me "all" out to the house for a nice pork roast and an evening of bourbon and talk, during the course of which he'd let it be known that I'd be better off not messin' in the little, old robbery I'd been assigned to investigate. And, when, in due course, the case petered out and nothing was recovered, Porky let it be known that his house was my house, whenever I saw fit to pay him a visit. He was mighty 'preciative. Mighty.

I hadn't made a habit of going over to Charles Street. But, the few times I had visited, Porky had come up with the name or the address of the man I was looking for. He was a rotund, seedy old man, with a shock of greasy straw-colored hair and the ragged look of a Kentucky colonel fallen on hard times. But he was a mine of information, and he was always mighty 'preciative to me.

It was three-thirty when I pulled up across from Porky's house on Charles Street. Mint julep time on the old veranda. I could see ten or twelve of his cronies on the porch and a half-dozen more chatting in groups on the stoop and the lawn. Red Bannion was among them. A compact, strong-armed man with a small town cop's creased and weary face, black horn-rim glasses, and the kind of burr hair cut that makes for a streak of bald flesh down the center of the skull, Red was Porky's right-hand man, his valet, his drinking companion, his chief-of-police during the Golden Deer days, and his bodyguard. He waved to me from the stoop as I walked up the lawn.

"Long time no see, lad," he said, shaking my hand vigorously. "Old Porky is going to be mighty glad you come."

Red guided me by the arm up to the veranda and hollered: "Hey, Porky! Y'all look who's come to see ya!"

"Harry!" Porky called from his rocker. "Harry Stoner!"

He made a half-hearted effort to work his enormous body out of the chair and I waved him back.

"Sit," he said to me, pointing to a chair beside him.

I sat.

He didn't look as if he'd changed a bit since I'd last talked to him, and I told him so. Still the same broad-faced, mopheaded old boy from Berea.

"No, Harry," he whined in a husky, whiskey-scented voice. "I'm changing, son. Getting up in *years*." Porky had a way of lingering over words, a finicky oratorical style of speaking that he'd probably picked up while politicking and kept up after he'd retired from public life because it mated so well with that country-squire life style. "To what do I owe the pleasure of this heah visit?"

"Business, Porky," I said to him.

"I figured," he said with a sigh. "When y'all goin' ta come over heah for somethin' other than *business?*"

I shrugged. "It can't be helped."

"Aw, shoot," he said. "That ain't so. Someday, boy, you're goin' ta wake up and discover that we ain't so different as you *think*. You know, we're all nigguhs under the skin, Harry. Some of us are a little *fatter* than most—" He broke up in hoarse laughter and waved it away with his chubby hands. "Okay," he said, clapping his knees. "What kin I do for ya?"

"I need some facts."

Porky's flat brown eyes flitted toward the men

standing along the railing of the veranda and then back to me. "Red!" he shouted. "Y'all take these fine genl'men 'round back, will ya? Show 'em the barbecue and where we hide the liquor."

The men along the railing chuckled feebly and began to file off the porch. Porky held up a fat hand of farewell and winked with his mouth. "I'll be 'round directly."

When the last of them had disappeared around the corner of the house, Porky's hand dropped to his lap and his mouth winked shut. "All right, Harry. What is it?"

I reached inside my coat and pulled out the three photographs of Cindy Ann. Porky looked at them for a minute, expressionlessly, and then winked with his mouth. "Hot, ain't it?" he said, fanning himself with the sheaf of snapshots. "Suppose to hit near a hunnert today." He handed the pictures back to me and folded his hands on his belly. "That ain't exactly in my line," he said.

"I *know* that," I said to him. "That's some old man's daughter, Porky. And all he wants is to get her back."

"An old man, you say?" Porky puckered his lips and plucked one of the photographs from my hand. "What exactly you need to know?"

"She's disappeared. I'd like to find out where. If she's been working this side of the river, I'd like to know that, too."

"What makes you think she's working over here?"

"A bird by the name of Abel Jones told me."

Porky winked twice.

"You know him?"

"I heard his name."

"Well, he and a pair of high-steppers named Jellicoe are somehow tied into this. They've got that girl. And you've seen the pictures."

He looked at the photo again. *"Shit.* She's just a kid." He shook his head and tut-tutted with his lips. "Times *do* change. Don't nobody I know right offhand go in for this sorta thing." He tucked the snapshot in his shirt and gaped at the lawn. "Red!" he bellowed.

Bannion came trundling around the side of the house, one hand pressed against his glasses and the other hovering nervously above the flap of his coat.

"Is old Willie Keeluh still runnin' the *theat-uh* over on Main Street?"

Red passed a hand over his brow and squinted up at the porch. "I think so," he said. "Yessuh, I think he is."

Porky got to his feet with a quickness that just didn't seem possible in a man of his size and years. "Y'all take Harry heah over ta see him. I'll go on back and keep them boys entertained."

Porky danced down the steps and out into the yard. "You keep in touch, heah?" he said to me. "I'll work on this for ya and let you know what I find."

Red Bannion drove me over to the theater in Porky's pink Cadillac. Around Porky, Red always seemed a genial man, quick to share in his employer's moods. In the car, he was silent and unfriendly and his weather-beaten face quickly assumed a look of undisguised boredom. I figured he didn't like to be sent on Porky's errands and, since I was the cause, I figured he didn't particularly like me. Red must have been sixty years old that summer, but, like Porky, there was a good deal of mean energy left in him. And I, for one, didn't want to get on the wrong side of it.

Willie Keeler's theater was located on North Main in a block that was taken up by small retail stores—shoe stores, furniture stores, laundromats. The marquee said that a flick called *Young and Restless* was playing, and it also said that "proof of age is strictly enforced." A couple of sad cases were loitering in front of the ticket window. Red shooed them away with a "Git!" and marched through the big glass doors. He was mad, all right. And I decided the quicker I could make this business the better for everyone. I didn't think Keeler would know much about the pictures, anyway. There's a limited market for the sort of thing those photos advertised. What I had to do was find one satisfied customer and then I might be able to work my way back through him to Cindy Ann.

There was a popcorn machine and a glass candy case in the lobby of the theater, and, to their right, was a wooden door marked "Office." Red didn't bother to knock. He just barged through the door, and I followed him in.

Keeler was a gaunt, silver-haired man in his early fifties with a slick sallow complexion that reminded me of a piece of wax fruit. He was sitting behind a small desk when we came through the door. He'd apparently been listening to a baseball game on a little table radio beside the desk. But he flipped it off as soon as we entered the room and stood up with a start, as if we'd caught him in flagrante delicto.

"Don't you know how to knock?" he snapped at Red. His voice was thin and nasal. Not the kind of voice that was comfortable snapping at a man like Red Bannion. I had the impression from the way Keeler was acting that, once, maybe not so long before, Red had gotten tough with him and had gotten away with it.

Bannion looked at him once, a cop's look, the kind of glance that's really a form of computation rather than an open-eyed stare. Then, his eyes shut down to slits and he said, "Porky sent us," in a matter-of-fact voice.

"Yeah?" Keeler looked at me uncertainly. "You're not the law, are you? Because if you are, I've paid my monthly dues. You can call Phil Tracewell over at C.I.D., if you don't believe me."

"I'm not the law. I'm a P.I., and I'm looking for a missing girl." I handed him one of the photos from my pocket. "This girl."

Keeler picked up a pair of bifocals that were laying on his desk and peered down at the picture as if he were reading the ingredients on a soup can label. "No," he said, shaking his head. He flipped off the glasses and handed the photo back to me. "I've never seen her."

"Do you run loops in the lobby?" I asked him.

"Yeah. We have two quarter machines."

"How often do you change the loops?"

"Every two weeks."

"Well, I'd appreciate it if you'd keep an eye out for that face. If you spot her, give me a call."

I gave him one of my cards and, after thinking it over for a second, told him to keep the snapshot.

"We don't get much of the kiddie stuff," he said. "The cops don't like it." He glared at Red Bannion and said, "Do they, Red?"

"I wouldn't know what cops like or don't like," he said flatly.

"The hell," Keeler said. "I'll keep an eye open, Stoner. Sometimes we get local stuff for the machines. If this one pops up, I'll let you know."

＝＝＝＝

Red Bannion's spirits improved considerably on the trip back to Charles Street.

"I don't like that man," he said cheerfully. "Don't care for that line of work at all."

We drove down Main to Seventh Street and past the Golden Deer. Red looked affectionately out the window as we passed by. "Hope you don't mind me comin' this way," he said. "Sometimes I just gotta remind myself who I am."

"No, Red. I don't mind," I said.

"Lad," he said wistfully. "You'd be plumb amazed at how things have changed in this town. When Porky and I started out after the war, there was only one club on Seventh Street. Now, look at it."

He waved his arm at the row of rococo night clubs—the Kittycat, the Silver Mule, the Hideaway, the Three-Ring Circus, the Dew Drop Inn.

"Looks like skid row, now, don't it? It's all gone bad and sneaky. It's all—commercial," he said with distaste. "No character anymore. Hell, you could line the men that run those joints up against a wall and you'd be hard put to tell one from the next. They're all of them wops in business suits and sunglasses. Not like the old days when it was Porky and Texas Jim McElroy and Hymie Gould. No," he said mournfully. "It's all changed."

There's nothing like a sentimental gangster to put the world in perspective. Red Bannion was working up to something. And, since he was not the kind of man to whom confession came easily, he'd prefaced it—whatever it was—with a short ride and a bit of old times, as if he were working off his inhibitions by reminding himself of who he had been and of who he was now. I thought maybe what he wanted to say had to do with Willie Keeler. The hatred that both men felt for each other had been obvious. I'd even thought of asking him about it when we'd stepped back out onto the sidewalk; but, thank God, some little warning bell went off in my head just as I was about to open my mouth. I suppose one of the hardest things I've had to learn in life is *not* to ask a detective's questions of my friends, which is damn tough to remember when you're usually getting paid to be nosy. As it turned out, it was a good thing I'd been able to keep my mouth shut, because what Red wanted to say had nothing to do with Keeler.

He pulled the Cadillac up across from the house on Charles Street and sat back in the seat with a sigh. He swiped off his glasses and tenderly massaged the indentations they'd made on the bridge of his nose. "Those pictures, Harry," he said in an achy voice. "Who wants to know about 'em?"

"An old man in Clifton," I said. "He's the girl's father."

Bannion nodded and continued to rub his nose. His eyes were shut and, for just a second, I had the eerie feeling he was praying. His teeth raked once across his lower lip, and he opened his eyes and pushed the glasses firmly back on his nose. In that split second, he'd come to some sort of decision about what he wanted to say and concluded that he could live with it, or, maybe, that *I* could. "I may be able to help you with this," he said, smiling at me. "Seems to me I done seen that girl's face some place before, though I'll be damned if I kin recollec' where. You wanna give me a look at one of those photos?"

I took the third print out of my coat and passed it over to Red. He flipped down the sun visor and held the snapshot in front of him. "Sure 'nough I seen this girl," he said. "In Newport, not too long ago. 'Course, she was made up different." He touched the air as if he were touching Cindy Ann's face. "Her hair was—" he swept the air into long tresses. "And her eyes was made up different, too. Shoot, in this picture, she don't look more'n sixteen."

"That's how old she is."

"Naw," Red said and flicked the snapshot with his thumbnail. "She gotta be older than that."

I looked at him a second and asked: "Why?"

Red flushed slightly and said, "No reason. No reason a'tall. Might not have been this girl, neither. We can check it out, though. Over at the Deer."

"Was she hooking, Red?" I said. "Is that what you're saying?"

He looked down at the dash. "I don't rightly know, Harry. We can check it out, though. Y'all wanna come back over heah tonight?"

"I can't tonight," I said.

"Well, maybe I kin give you a call tomorrow morning. And let you know if it was her I saw. Kin I keep this?" he said, holding up the photo.

"Yeah."

"You still in Clifton?"

"Still and always."

"All rightie," he said and opened the car door. We got out, and Red straightened himself and brushed at his coat. "I don't like that kind of thing," he said and smiled without pleasure. "Me and ol' Willie had us some words about it no more'n a year or so ago. I'd like to lend a hand, if I could. If you don't mind?"

He looked up at me and smiled like a choir boy. A brawny, yellow-toothed, bullet-headed, sixty-year-old choir boy.

"I don't mind," I told him.

# 10

**THE SUN WAS** setting behind me as I crossed the Suspension Bridge, but the day's heat was still cooking the air. The nightfall was sticky hot and the evening would remain hot long past midnight. It was those damn hills that did it; they contained the heat like the walls of an oven and, with it, the fumes of the downtown industries and the exhaust of the cars and buses. I hadn't heard the news but I guessed that pollution was near the alert level. A sickly bile-colored haze was floating above the river and laying in fog-like patches along the basin. I felt tired and sweaty-dirty, as if I'd spent the afternoon baling hay instead of talking with three local mobsters.

Time to go home, Harry, I told myself. Time to take accounts and plan tomorrow's fun. A meeting with the Jellicoes would be in order. But a nice pressureless one. A gab session, with Harry the Venal

Detective speaking lightly of old men clients and young missing girls and the very off-chance of some sort of unexpected trouble cropping up. Some photos maybe. Not that it all couldn't be smoothed over with a few dollars and a bit of cooperation. I couldn't risk much more than a veiled threat. After what Coral had said, even that might be too much. But it had to be done sooner or later. I decided that I'd need the photos anyway, even if I didn't flash them at Lance and Laurie. And since I'd exhausted my supply, that meant another stop at the bus depot.

I turned off the expressway at Front Street and slid down through the concrete ramping onto Columbia Parkway and immediately nosed back up again, like a shallow-diving seal, and broke back into the night at the Vine Street overpass. Behind me, Riverfront Stadium glowed like a squat Japanese lantern. I turned north in front of it and headed up into the dense wall of red brick buildings that is the beginning of the city. Along Fountain Square the street lamps popped on—that dried-out shade of green that's almost white. And the store lights and office lights began to burnish the darkening sky. I turned east at Fifth and drove back down through Government Square to the bus terminal where I had seen Hugo off ages before.

I was lucky enough to find a parking place on Elm. Lucky because it was a Saturday night in July and most folks preferred to spend it in a bar or a theater rather than at home in front of the T.V. The sidewalks were crowded with ladies in their pastels and their gentlemen in lightweight suits of beige and sky-blue. I felt like a toad, hopping among them in my day-old shirt and slacks and in my twill seersucker sports coat that looked as if it had been scored by a truck tire. But, hell—I was too tired to care. Except, maybe, for the ladies. I liked the ladies. I liked the way they moved under their gauzy dresses. I liked the look of their shoulders in the night. And of their legs as their arms brushed against the flowing skirts. And of their dark eyes shot with white street light or with the warm golden light of the storefronts. God almighty! I said to myself, it *has* been awhile.

The bus station was what I really needed. I needed to be jarred by the candle-power of those countless lights, so many and from so many different angles that I don't think a giant could have cast a shadow in the Greyhound Bus Station. And I guess I needed another look at those merry souls waiting on the benches. Needed to hear once again the tap dance of my feet and the rasp of the loudspeaker—if it *was* a loudspeaker and not just a man who sounded like a loudspeaker. What I needed most of all was the pimply teenage boy who swished by me as I was getting the shoe box out of the locker and, propping one arm coyly against the repository, gazed down at me and pointed his foot like a dancer priming for a *grand jeté*.

"Hi," he said sweetly.

I shook my head. "Sorry, Bruce. You're pitching in the wrong league."

"I catch, too," he said cheerfully and danced away.

I felt like Hugo Cratz when I got back to my feet. Which reminded me—where the hell *was* Hugo Cratz? I tucked the shoe box under my arm and went looking for a pay phone. I found one next to a pinball arcade near the Elm Street exit. But it was one of those half-ass, exposed stands, without doors or seat or light. I've always felt that using one of those things was like buying a matching vest without the suit; except for emergencies, they're useless and about as private as a ghetto partyline.

I skulked back into the night and tried to watch the pavement and not to think about the laughter and the perfume and the bright-eyed ladies who were everywhere around me. Look at it this way, Harry, I told myself, sure they look good to you now. And, maybe, once you get past the gauze, they'd look better still. Brown where the sun has touched them and white and furry where it hasn't. . . . That line of argument was getting me nowhere. I started thinking about Jo Riley, about the way she looked when she dropped one knee on my bed and stretched the other out behind her in a svelte white line. I thought about the way her hair gathered on her shoulders and about the way her breasts swayed slightly as she breathed. Where the sun had tanned them they looked as if they began slightly lower on her chest than they really did, and their pink nipples seemed off-centered, set where the flesh became full and rounded and flowed beneath them in a milk-white curve.

She would probably be off around twelve. And I hadn't eaten. And, hell, everybody sweats when it's hot.

When I got to the Pinto, I headed due north, to Ludlow and the gray cube of the Busy Bee.

———

Once I'd gotten the fun part out of my system, I remembered the other half of that argument I'd been having with myself down by the bus depot. For there was no mistaking that she was another person, sleeping next to me. Small beneath the sheet, formulating and reformulating the marvelous topography of a woman's body as she turned from her dreams and sighed an easy, peaceful sigh, she was Jo. Jo of the coal-black hair and soft, heart-shaped, Mediterranean face. With all of Jo's wit, and Jo's powerful laugh, and Jo's driving independence. Jo, who could be as sweet as marzipan, and Jo who could be as hard and unyielding as . . . as Jo. But, by God, it *had* been worth it. Tickling up the stairs of the old Delores at two in the morning, drunk and acting drunk and festive-sly, like gate-crashers at a fabulous feast. Leaning on each other—the college kids. Pulling away with barks of laughter—the knowing adults. Coming in the door and staring silently, familiarly at the room and at each other. Feeling a bit of fear, then, when it was just Jo and

Harry and no one else. And when both Jo and Harry knew full well that what was going to happen was a beginning of something that had to end in a vow or a broken promise. Thank God, the appetites are faster and shrewder than the mind, or else there wouldn't have been Jo and Harry naked and famished for each other. And a great deal of tender and passionate embrace.

After the lovemaking, I'd sat back against the headboard, arms behind my head, and wondered why on earth I had once thought this would never work. Then, late in the evening, when the air was cooled by a sudden breeze that flushed through the apartment, I remembered why. I remembered that core of reserve, that sudden toughness that would change her into a stranger in a place that I shared no part of. Remembered the admiration I'd felt for that tough-minded independence. And the guilty sense of relief, because that reserve was like an assurance that things could only go so far and no farther, that there would always be that piece of her I couldn't share. A buffer zone. A moat. How good it had made me feel until, one afternoon, I'd discovered that what she kept there, behind the moat, was her heart.

It was the detective that did me in. Rummaging, exploring, running hands and eyes over a drawerful of her things—jewelry, make-up, a heart-shaped watch on a golden chain, a Japanese fan, some silk underwear, and, in the back, buried beneath the panties, the hard corner of a photograph set in a cardboard frame. I flicked it with my finger, teased it with my eye. And, finally, I pulled it out. It was a wedding picture of a very young Jo and of a tow-headed Marine corporal with his cap buttoned on his shoulder and a loose grin on his face. She caught me with it in my hand.

She walked over to the dresser and pulled the photograph away and tucked it back in with the underwear.

"Why didn't you tell me?" I asked her.

"I suppose because I didn't want you to know."

"It doesn't make a difference."

"It does to me," she said, closing the drawer. "We're still married."

And then I got what I'd angled for, told patiently, unblushingly, by this strong, black-haired woman with the bridge-club spectacles and the pretty, heart-shaped face. He was an M.I.A., her corporal husband, whom she hadn't seen in five years and whom she still loved enough to cry over with regret.

When she was done, I wandered off into the living room and fumed at myself and called myself a dictionary full of dirty names. And, in a few minutes, she came in, too, and curled up beside me and said, "Now, you know," in her husky voice. "Can't love anybody else. Not for awhile. Maybe not ever. Not until I've gotten over him. You're the closest I've come, though. Real close. Only when I think I'm almost there with you, it's not you I'm thinking of. And that scares me."

A few weeks later we'd told each other goodbye. Both of us, I think, feeling relieved that we wouldn't have to carry the affair any further, that that moat wouldn't have to be crossed and the keep inside taken by storm. Or not taken.

But, that hot July night, with Jo sleeping beside me again after three years of absence, I suddenly felt infinitely more valorous. Maybe it was the box of photographs sitting on the living room coffee table. Or the thought of the totally loveless and carnal act they pictured. Or the memory of the Jellicoes. Because those are the folks that never cross moats and carry castles, Harry, I thought. They're the sick by-products of a selfish and unromantic age. And you can either line yourself up on their side and pretend indignance. Or you can try to love the woman lying beside you and take the risk of being hurt.

But not of being hurt like Cindy Ann was hurt. Not brutalized like a thing. I tried to picture that sixteen-year-old girl-child in a hiked-up skirt with white plastic boots on her legs and a pound of pan-cake and mascara on her face, hooking the tough bar rail of the Golden Deer. It was just possible. Per-haps the Jellicoes had given up on her. Or, perhaps, she was only acting as bait. Or, maybe, Red Bannion had an old man's eyes and sixty years of guilty con-science and a desperate urge to make a few amends. The morality of an old hoodlum is like a Baptist's notion of charity—a kind of fervent embarrassment.

I touched Jo on the shoulder and she rolled into

my arms. That was best. By far. And I fell asleep, holding her and that thought in my arms.

The telephone woke me at eight the next morning—far earlier than I'd wanted to be awakened. I tried to ignore it until Jo mumbled something about not waking her, too. So I stumbled out of bed, stark naked, and padded into the living room. It must have been close to ninety in the goddamn room, and it was too early to start the day, and I heartily wished that whoever was calling me was in hell. I got to the phone on the tenth ring and yelled, "What!" into the receiver.

"Is this Harold . . . Stoner?" a high-pitched, uncertain voice inquired.

I sat down on the desk chair, wiped the sweat from my face, and laughed out loud.

"Harry?"

"Yes . . . Hugo," I said. "It's me."

"Good," he said. " 'Cause for a minute there I thought I'd dialed the wrong number. I left my specs back at the apartment and the print in these here phonebooks is so damn small—"

"What time is it, Hugo?"

"Why, it's eight. Or thereabouts."

"Eight in the morning?"

"Sure."

I blew a little steam out of my mouth and said, "How's Dayton?"

"It stinks," Hugo said dully. "Just like I thought

**111**

it would. Them snot-nosed brats of Ralph's was up in my room every damn minute. Couldn't sleep a wink last night. That's why I called you."

I guess you pay, one way or another, for what you do. Ralph's kids wake Hugo, Hugo wakes me. At least he was in Dayton and out of harm's way. "You'll manage," I said to him.

"Hell, yes, I'll manage. That's easy for you to say. I'm a sick man, Harry. Last night, that youngest one kicked me so hard in the spine, I thought I'd dropped a kidney. I won't last up here," he said tragically. "No, sir, I'm a dead man. You're talking to a dead man, Harry Stoner. And you're the one that sent him to his grave."

"C'mon, Hugo. You'll make it."

"I will, will I?" He took a breath and chuckled. "Maybe I will. But there's some others that may not. When you going to let me come back?"

"A couple of days, maybe," I said, thinking about what Red Bannion had told me. "It depends on how things go."

"You talk to them Jellicoes, yet?"

"No. I spent yesterday trying to find out what they had Cindy Ann doing."

"Did you find out?"

I hesitated for a minute before telling him and decided that he was tough enough to hear the truth. Without it, he'd be impossible to handle. And he was going to have to hear it, anyway, sooner or later. "They may have her working as a prostitute in Newport."

"Oh, God," he said faintly.

"Easy, Hugo. If she is working as a hooker, I have friends who can spot her and get her back to us. I'll know tonight for sure."

"You'll call me?"

"Yes."

"She ain't . . . they ain't abusing her, are they? I mean like in them pictures?"

"I don't think so," I said.

" 'Cause I couldn't stand that, Harry. That would do me for sure."

He asked if I'd call him, again, and I told him I would, again. He started to get trembly, and I told him everything was going to be fine. Then he said he was counting on me. And he hung up.

I was feeling a very different kind of weariness as I trudged back to the bedroom. If Jo hadn't been sleeping so soundly, I would have tried to ease the load by confessing some of it to her. The big difference between detectives in books and detectives in real life is that detectives in books are always rescuing their clients from perilous straits—which is a bunch of hokum and dangerous hokum, at that. That's the way we would have things be, when the bitter truth is that no one can rescue anyone from anything. As exciting and professional as they are, those books about ageless beach bums who salvage their women's psyches along with the family fortunes aren't doing the world much good. All it takes is a little living to know how far from the truth that kind of fantasy can lead you and how irresponsible and finally dehumanizing playing the role of rescuer can be.

Now, I am and have always been a sentimentalist. I'm a sucker for romance, maybe because I have so much trouble conjuring it up in my own life or maybe because it's more romantic to live it out through other people's lives. But, in my work, there comes a time when I have to abandon the abiding and pleasant notion that Harry can make it all come out right in the end. Harry can't do that. And Harry shouldn't promise desperate old men that he can. And Harry shouldn't take jobs with that in mind. And Harry was feeling sick at what he'd committed himself to. And thinking that the trouble with charity work is not the pay but the working conditions. That they're too damn unreal. And Harry wanted a shoulder of his own to cry on. But the only shoulder available belonged to the slender and beautiful young woman lying next to him, who might or might not be willing to serve as a hankie, but whom Harry was not certain he had the right to infringe on. If, indeed, it was infringement and not just plain old human need, which was also something Harry was unsure of. And he fell asleep feeling unsure about it, while, at the same time, regretting not having told Hugo Cratz what Hugo Cratz already knew —that there was a good chance that, even if she could be pried from the Jellicoes in one piece, Cindy Ann would probably never want to see that sour, old man's apartment again.

# 11

THE SECOND TIME I awoke that morning the bells of St. Anne's were sounding sext. I rolled over in the bed and brushed a lock of black hair from Jo's face.

"Sunday," I said and kissed her lightly on the lips.

She opened her eyes and smiled at me. There was sunlight in the western windows, and the bedroom was hot and bright. Her face looked almost wan in the white sunlight and sleepy-pretty. "Sunday," she said dreamily and rolled out of bed.

I showered and shaved while Jo made coffee in the little cubicle off the living room—the "kitchenette" as Robert Realty calls it. What it is is a shelfless pantry with a two-burner stove on one wall, a midget refrigerator on another, and an aluminum sink crammed in between. There's just enough space for a normal-sized human being to stand amid them, though it's rather like standing in the U of a U-shaped control console. Moreover, since I'm slightly larger than normal size, I have to stoop a bit and sidle in an out of the U if I want to, say, turn from the refrigerator to the stove. It makes cooking and washing dishes a challenge, which is why I generally eat out.

There was something pleasantly domestic about having Jo in there doing the sidling and turning. Although I couldn't help thinking as I towelled off and stared critically at my lumpy, unshaven face— the face of a busted Roman statue, as a romantic lady-friend once put it—that there was something fairly fragile about the little sounds of satisfaction and frustration she was making in the kitchenette. And from the way my own hand was shaking, I understood why. You can't kid the heart, cajole it the way you would a temperamental child. It'll have its say, regardless. But you can't hurry it, either. And, as the morning progressed, as those nighttime resolutions melted away in the sun and the seasonableness of everyday living, it was getting harder and harder for the heart to say what it wanted to say, without stuttering and blushing and holding a finger to its lips. Too much longer and it might not speak at all. And that was why I was shaking and Jo was sounding fragile and sad.

I was almost relieved when the phone rang.

"I'll get it," I shouted.

I walked into the bedroom, picked up the extension and said, "Stoner."

"Harry, this is Red Bannion. I've got some news that'll interest you."

I sat down on the mattress and dabbed with the sheet at my wet face. "Like what, Red?"

"That girl," he said. "I jus' knew I'd seen her before. And I was right. Ol' Bill Hallan who works the bar at the Deer says he seen her more'n half a dozen times. But she ain't no free-lance hooker. Everytime she come in, she come in with somebody different. And once she come in with somebody real special. Does the name Preston LaForge mean anything to you?"

I didn't say a thing for a second. "You're shitting me, aren't you, Red?"

"Naw, sir, I ain't. Last time she come in the Deer, Bill Hallan says she was with LaForge."

"I don't believe it," I said, half to myself.

"It do seem strange," Red mused. "Don't seem like a man like that would cozy up to a kid like her. Not with his connections."

I guess you never know about people in the public eye. From what I'd seen of him, Preston LaForge seemed like the all-American boy. An all-star in college. A rookie sensation with the Bengals and a perennial all-pro. He was barely thirty and a rich man, a popular man, with a rock-solid future in national broadcasting ahead of him once he'd quit the pros. His pink, chubby, boyish face was already familiar from after-shave ads and beer commercials. And, during the post season, he'd been in the color commentary booth joking and gabbing with Merlin Olson. It shook me a little to think that a man like that would go for green fruit, and bruised fruit, at that. And I think it shook me a little more to think that Preston LaForge didn't have brains enough to keep his bad habits to himself.

But it did make a kind of bizarre sense that he would end up with Cindy Ann on his arm, especially if she was working for the Jellicoes. Ol' Lance was certainly the pro-football type. And I'd seen him working out at the Nautilus Club, where many of the Bengals keep in shape. It wasn't hard to picture him and Preston going out for a drink, maybe stopping at the Jellicoes' apartment for some smoke and talk and a peek at the family album.

"Two more things," Bannion said. "I got me a name—Escorts Unlimited. Seems like that's the outfit your youngster was workin' for. They're on Plum Street, but I'd be willin' to bet there ain't nothin' in the office but an answerin' machine."

I jotted down the name "Escorts Unlimited" on a pad. "What's the other thing?" I said to him.

Bannion made a small, tired noise—a sort of unambitious sigh—that came out "hem." Then he said, "She ain't been around in near a week, and she was showing up pretty regular before that. Or so Bill Hallan tells me."

I made a little "hem" of my own. "That's not so good," I said.

"I didn't like it none, either. 'Course she could've been cut loose. Those things happen. Or she could've gone off on her own."

"At sixteen?"

"Oh, hell, Harry," Bannion said wearily. "She's sixteen goin' on forty. She probably ain't got an unused part left."

I thought of Hugo Cratz and bit softly at my lip. "Well, thanks, Red. You've been a big help."

"Hold on, Harry," he said. "Don't you go off half-cocked on this one, lad. This is sixty hard years talking to you, now. This boy LaForge is bound to have him some mean friends. And those folks runnin' that escort service ain't likely to be play-school children neither. You tangle with them, Harry, and they're goin' to kill you, lad. You'd be best advised to forget this whole thing. Just chalk 'er up on the wrong side. And tell that poor old man to forget her. He don't know it, but he'd probably be better off not findin' out what become of her."

I didn't say anything.

"How much is that man payin' you?" Red said in his achy voice. "Couldn't be near enough to cover the risk of somethin' like this."

I laughed hollowly. "Nothing," I said. "I'm doing it for nothing."

"Then, boy you're as crazy as a loon if you don't drop this whole damn thing right now. Listen to Red. I been through it and I know. Ain't nothin' worth gettin' killed for."

"Nothing," I said dully.

"Nothin' you hired yourself out to do," Red Bannion said. "A man don't take wages for his life."

After hanging up, I thought a few minutes about

the things a man *does* take wages for. A man like
Lance Jellicoe and a man like Preston LaForge. But,
somehow, I just couldn't work up any real indignation. That angry little man who'd gotten me into
this mess in the first place was deliberately looking
the other way now, with his hands clasped behind
his back and his toe swivelling in the dirt and a
sheepish grin frozen on his red face.

"Cindy Ann," I said out loud and it came out
sounding like a curse.

"Harry?" Jo called from the living room. "Did
you say something?"

"No. Didn't say anything."

"Come on in and have some coffee."

I wrapped a robe around me and walked into
the living room, where Jo was lounging in the recliner next to the Zenith Globemaster. She was
wearing a cup of coffee in her right hand.

I let my eyes travel up and down that magnifi-
cent body. She looked so damn good to me at that
moment, so ripe and uncomplicated and full of
health that I almost shouted. Her breasts were flattened a bit because she was lying back in the chair.
She had one leg on the cushion and the other
stretched to the floor. When she saw the look on my
face, she smiled and brought the other leg up and,
leaning forward and clasping her knees, propped
her chin on her kneecaps and stared speculatively at
me. She'd have looked like a kid stealing a last
glimpse of a movie from the back of a theater, save

for the firm, round, throat-tightening curve of her breast and the very naked flesh between her thighs.

"So," she said. "We're back together, now."

"I'm glad," I said and meant it.

"I can see that," she said with a little laugh and ducked her head. "So am I, Harry. I kept waiting for it. Sometimes I'd start to say something myself." She looked boldly up at me. "I think it could work this time. At least, I'm willing to give it a try."

"Right now?" I said.

She put her coffee cup down next to the Globemaster and, rising to her feet, walked gracefully over to me and tugged at the loose cord of the bathrobe. "Right now," she said.

———

I didn't want the day to start.

I didn't want to think about anything but Jo. No Hugo Cratzes, no Lance and Laurie Jellicoes, no Cindy Anns, no Preston LaForges.

It was the lady herself who brought me back to reality with a feathery kiss. I felt her weight shift on the mattress, and then she was gone.

"Hey!" I said. "Where're you going?"

She looked slyly over her shoulder and said, "I'll be back. I've got a few errands to run. And a few things to pack. Like toothbrush, comb, change of clothes. A girl scout kit for grown-up girl scouts." She walked into the john and, in a minute, I could hear the hiss of the shower.

I lay back on the bed and bellowed. Jo laughed. *"Roar!"* she shouted over the shower.

At half-past two, Jo kissed me and marched to the front door. She'd put on her disguise for the trip out—the bridge-club spectacles, the bee-hive hairdo, the subdued plaid secretary's suit.

"You can't fool me!" I called out from the bedroom.

"Beneath this mask of tragedy," she said, pivoting at the door, "is a leering face. I'll see you around six."

*"Vale,"* I said and sank back into the bed.

I spent about five minutes shuffling a deck of cards, five minutes browsing through the Sunday paper, five more changing channels on the T.V., five just staring at the ceiling. And then I yanked the phonebook from the nightstand and looked up Escorts Unlimited.

It was a quaint address for an escort service, right in the middle of the wholesale garment district on lower Plum. Just for the hell of it, I gave Escorts Unlimited a call. I got a pleasant recorded message telling me that no one was in the office at that moment and directing me to phone a different number after six. I jotted down the second number and, just for the hell of it, looked up the Jellicoes' phone number in the directory. They weren't listed.

Those "just-for-the-hell-of-its" were wearing thin. But it was a hot, sleepy Sunday and I didn't have anything else to do. So, just for the hell of it, I went ahead and placed a call to an old friend at Ma Bell. And, sure enough, she came up with the Jellicoes' home number.

It was identical to the one the recording had referred me to. After six, at least, the Jellicoes *were* Escorts Unlimited. And I had the feeling the Escorts Unlimited only operated after six.

I doodled on the note pad, and pretended that what Bannion had told me hadn't shaken my resolve. What we had was one very young girl, venal and possibly crazy. Certainly well and variously used, as Red had pointed out. And, from the look of it, perfectly happy in her work. Then we had two rather unusual pimps, an attractive, middle-class couple, venal and possibly crazy themselves, who might or might not run a legitimate escort service but who certainly catered to rather kinky customers on the side. And, then, we had one professional football player—wide-receiver, to be precise. Six-two, eyes of blue, sandy hair, cherubic face, all the money and prestige he could want, and a taste for little girls whom he could poke and prod like when he was a kid playing "Doctor." Just your typical American grouping. And what family would be complete without the old 'un. And, yet, Hugo, for all his chicanery, despite his unwashed, seedy self, didn't seem to fit in. The dirty old man outdirtied by a congeries of more or less respectable types. What a good one on the dirty old men. What a good laugh the clean-cut ones would have. Except, perhaps, for

Cindy Ann, who wasn't so clean and was temporarily vanished into the dark and grisly night world of Newport.

Would she resurface? Would Hugo Cratz live to see his "little girl" returned to him? Not likely. And not funny, either. It would "do" him, all right—to hear the truth. He'd blow an artery when he was told. Or, maybe, he wouldn't. Maybe he'd go out and dummy another P.I. into hunting up his Cindy Ann. He wasn't going to get what was left of her back on his own. He'd need some truly professional prying and finagling for that.

I threw the note pad down on the nightstand and got to my feet. It wouldn't do to try the photos out on the Jellicoes after what Red had told me. They just wouldn't bite. As long as Cindy Ann was missing, they could stick to their story and no one could prove they weren't telling the gospel truth. No one could prove that they had taken the photos in the first place. An operation like theirs was bound to be fairly well insulated. Layers of lawyers and business contacts and witnesses who would swear the Jellicoes were allergic to SX-70 film and, if things got really tough, strong-arm hoods like Abel Jones who would make me eat the film and the camera, too, and then shove a tripod up my ass and hire me out for studio work. But, a good ol' boy like Preston LaForge, with those little gobs of apple pie still sticking to his lips and those blue, blue eyes and that all-American face—*he* I could work on, because he had *everything* to lose if those pictures found their way to the police. And, happily enough, Preston had a listed number and an address in the swell part of Mt. Adams.

# 12

THE VICARAGE IS a multi-leveled complex of condo-
miniums set on a steep hillside overlooking the
Ohio. From below, it looks rather pleasantly like a
gigantic redwood aviary propped on telephone
poles. From the entrance on Celestial, it has the luxe
and manicured look of a well-run apartment. There
is a small cobbled courtyard from which the condos
radiate out in a broad semicircle. Here and there, a
paved avenue carries back into the complex itself.
The apartments are A-frame, chalet-like buildings—
mostly tilted redwood roof and plate glass. I'd been
in one of them once, at a posh reception I was hired
to oversee, and the best thing about it had been the
view from the porch. The interior was groined and
vaulted like a church—a great, high-ceilinged dead
space filled with rich, bored people, handsome furniture, and tasteless objets d'art. I wouldn't have let

my lease on the Delores expire to move in there; but, then, the chances of me being invited to move into the Vicarage were very slim. It was, in fact, peopled by invitation only. And, only the choicest people were invited. Johnny Bench lived there. Thomas Schippers, when he was alive, had lived there. The Gambles of P & G had a little retreat on the hillside. And so did Preston LaForge.

I parked the Pinto in a stall marked *Visitors* and walked out of the sunlit courtyard and through a sweet-smelling tunnel of weathered cedar to the door of LaForge's apartment. There were plexiglass inserts in the tunnel, looking out above the green hillside toward the blue reach of the Ohio. It was an impressive sight, but all I could think about was how mean a drop it would be to tumble off one of the rough-hewn porches that terraced the hill. And that's exactly where I could find myself if Preston LaForge didn't fancy the picture I was going to show him or the idea of being blackmailed into helping me find Cindy Ann. I patted the gun in my pocket and raised my hand to the door.

LaForge answered on the first knock. He'd been waiting for someone and his big grin died when he saw that it was only me. He had to be over thirty but he looked barely nineteen, with the sensuous blonde face of the California beach boy. Behind him, the room seemed to climb and climb. The far wall was one great triangle of glass and a huge triangle of white sunlight fell through it, setting the cream shag rug and the chrome and glass and brass furnishings ablaze.

I shaded my eyes and said, "Do you have to wear sunglasses to live in there?"

LaForge giggled. And I don't mean laughed. I mean giggled. A kid's chortle that, in all decency, should have been covered with a hand before it left his mouth. "That's *funny!*" he said all agog. "That's really funny! Do you mind if I use that myself?"

"Feel free," I said.

"Say, who the hell are you, anyway?" he said affably. "You want a drink?" He just walked away from the door, leaving it wide open and me standing on the stoop. "I got liquor here somewhere," he said, rummaging a glass-and-chrome tea cart parked on the south wall beneath what looked like a genuine Mondrian. "Sunglasses!" he chuckled. "I'll have to tell Oscar that. He's the fag that decorated this place." LaForge turned to me, a pair of ice tongs in his hands. "You know they write that in the lease? You've got to have a fag decorator come in and camp the place up or they won't rent to you. Bourbon, O.K.?" he said, dropping the ice with a clunk into a cut-glass goblet.

"Sure," I said and walked right on in.

"I'm a Scotch man myself," he said over the drinks. "But I ran out last night. Like the man said, though. Between bourbon and nothing, I'll take bourbon." He picked up the glasses and brought them over to where I was standing. "Pull up a chair," he said, handing me a glass.

We sat down on opposite ends of a big gray leather sofa. LaForge stretched out and slopped a little bourbon on one of the cushions.

"Damn," he said. "Oscar's going to kill me when he sees this." He chuckled and made a half-hearted effort to wipe off the spot with his shirt-sleeve. "Does leather stain?" he said. "I mean does bourbon stain leather?"

"Damned if I know."

LaForge stopped wiping and looked up at me as if he'd just noticed I was in the room. "Say," he said pleasantly. "Who the hell are you? Or did I ask you that already?"

"You did."

"Oh," he said vaguely. He sipped at his drink and stared darkly at the floor. "I'm sorry, but I just don't have a good memory for names. Who did you say you were?"

"Stoner. Harry Stoner."

"Oh, yeah." LaForge smiled again and nodded equably. "What paper are you with, Harry?"

"I'm not with a paper, Mr. LaForge."

"Oh, hell, call me Preston. Everybody does." A gloomy look passed across his boyish face. "All my life, they've been calling me Preston," he said remotely. Whatever it had been, it was gone in a second. "Better than Johnny, huh? Why the hell do baseball players always have names ending with 'ee'? Johnny, Davey, Jackie, Bucky . . ."

"Dopey, Sleepy . . ."

LaForge giggled again. "Say, I like you, you

know that? You're a funny guy. You sure you don't write for a paper or a magazine? Oh, hell, I guess you'd know that, wouldn't you?"

He sipped at his drink again. "So, what can I do for you?"

I stared at him a minute. In amazement. "This isn't an act, is it, Preston?" I said.

"What?" he said and his face made ready to laugh again.

"I mean this incredibly affable, dumb, schoolboy bit. That's the real you, isn't it?"

He shrugged. "I guess."

"Well," I said with a mild laugh. "Then I just don't understand it."

He started to giggle. "What?"

"I mean, how did it happen? Did your daddy slip it to sis while you were watching? Did the school marm make you stand in the corner in wet pants? And did all the little girls laugh at you?"

LaForge knitted his bland brow. "What are you talking about?" he said cheerfully.

"Well . . . this." I pulled a snapshot of Cindy Ann out of my pocket and tossed it over to his side of the couch. He spilled a little more of his drink flagging it down.

"Damn," he said. "Does bourbon stain wool?" He toed at the carpet and glanced at the snapshot. "Oh, God," he said quietly and dropped his drink quite completely on the couch.

"You'd better clean that one up, Preston," I said. "That'll surely leave a stain."

He brushed fecklessly at the cushion and continued to stare at the photograph. I could see what was going to happen, and I felt bad for him.

"Poor thing," Preston LaForge said and his little boy's mouth trembled. "Poor, poor thing."

He began to cry, chewing his lips and staring vacantly at the picture of Cindy Ann. "I'm going to be sick," he said.

"I wouldn't do it on the rug, Preston."

He dropped the photo, got up, and ran agilely across the big cathedral-like room to a hallway that angled off next to the door. He disappeared down it and, in a second, I heard the sound of his retching and the flush of the toilet.

I was feeling a little sick myself and sad. But not for Preston. I'd gotten over that as soon as he'd started to cry. Like anything too sweet, Preston LaForge was cloying. I was feeling sad for Hugo. Because it seemed apparent, now, that something pretty terrible and pretty final had befallen his "little girl."

In a few minutes, LaForge came back down the hall. He looked awful. His face was a sick, bloodless white and his wrists seemed to dangle from his cuffs as if they were sewn to the cloth. "This is terrible," he said miserably. "What the hell am I going to do?" He looked at me helplessly.

"You wanna tell me about her, Preston?" I said.

He plopped down on a slung leather chair and held his face in his hands. "What's to tell. Her name is Cindy Ann Evans. She's sixteen. I . . ." He lowered his hands and stared forlornly at my face. "You know all this. Why do you want me to say it?"

"I'm looking for her. Her father wants her back."

"Oh, Christ." LaForge shook his head and sobbed. "I've got this . . . this thing," he said weakly. "I don't know where it comes from. I really don't." He took a deep breath and steadied himself. "I've been to psychiatrists. I'm seeing one now. It has to do with my mom. With the way she . . . she overprotected me. Dressed me up, you know?" He took another deep breath. "I only saw Cindy a couple of times. I swear to God, it was only a couple of times. I knew I was being bad, but I just . . . I can't help it." LaForge broke down again in tears.

"What happened to the girl?" I said to him.

He shook his head. "Don't know." LaForge wiped his eyes. "She was a nice kid. Sweet in a way. They had her on drugs. Half the time I don't think she knew what was going on. And the other half . . . she didn't seem to mind."

"Who are they?"

"What!" he said in alarm.

"The ones that had her on drugs."

"Oh. Laurie and Lance. They run a little service."

I got up from the couch and walked over to the big picture window and stared blankly down the hillside. He'd taken a lot and he'd spoken freely, irrepressibly, as if he were glad of the chance to say it. Some men are like that. They suffer remorselessly from what the French call *délire de confesser*. But this was the critical part, and as pitiable as Preston's good boy-bad boy personality was I wanted to make the hard truth stick.

"You've got a big future ahead of you, Preston. Big money, prestige, a family. I'd hate to see it all go down the drain."

"How much?" he said dully.

I turned around. With his arms on the armrests and his feet dangling to the floor and his face red and tear-stained, he looked like a hapless, crucified child. "I don't want money. I want to get Cindy Ann back. And, if that isn't possible, I want to find out what happened to her."

"That's it?" he said. "That's all?"

"Not quite. I want the Jellicoes, too. I want to put them out of business. Permanently."

"What am I supposed to do?"

"You're going to call Lance up. You're going to tell him you got a 'thing' for Cindy Ann. You're going to arrange a date."

"What if . . . I mean what if she isn't around?"

"You're not going to take no for an answer, Preston."

"You don't understand," LaForge said. "The Jellicoes . . . they run a safe business. That's how come people like me go to them. They guarantee safety. The girls are always . . . safe. You know? They're homeless. And you never see the same girl more than a couple of times."

"That's your problem, Preston," I said to him. "I

don't care how you do it. But you either bring Cindy Ann to me or you find out where she is."

LaForge started to say something but I cut him off. "You *do* it, Preston. Because if you don't, I'm going to take that picture and ruin you with it. They're going to put you in jail. And do you know what they do to sweet young things like you in jail, Preston? Man, they'll eat you alive. So, get cracking, Preston." I took a card from my wallet and tossed it on the rug. "You call me tonight at that number when you've got it arranged. And remember this— I've got twenty-five more pictures just like that one and every damn one is going to the cops if you double-cross me. And with them goes enough of a deposition about you and Cindy Ann and the Jellicoes to get a grand jury working overnight."

I started for the door. "As the man said, you'll thank me for this some day, Preston."

I heard him laughing stupidly as I walked out.

# 13

I **FELT SORRY** for Preston LaForge. He was a sad little boy trapped in a world that has no use for the weak or the winless. On any given day I might have tried to help him—the way I was helping Hugo at that very moment. But I would never be able to trust him the way I trusted Hugo. He just wasn't sane enough for that.

So I didn't leave the Vicarage right away. Instead, I got in the Pinto and waited, hunching down in the car seat and peering up at the rearview mirror.

And, sure enough, at half-past five, Preston popped into view.

He was dressed a little too carefully for a stroll—in a Ralph Lauren western outfit. Striped cowboy shirt, designer jeans, red scarf and topsiders. He looked like a picture from the sporting-wear section of a Neiman-Marcus catalogue. There was even something of the sportsman in the set of his face— the kind of martial alertness that hunters show when they're about to shoulder a gun. It occurred to me that that pretty beach boy was on the prowl. Perhaps out to prove that he could still have his way after I'd slapped his wrists and said, "No." It would be an understandable enough impulse in a man like him.

He walked across the lot to a Jaguar two-seater and glanced quickly at the sky before hopping in. It was clouding up overhead. A thick porridge of a sky. And I said a little prayer for rain as I started the Pinto and followed Preston out of the Vicarage lot.

It was cooler on the streets, with the storm brewing up. The air had a nervous thrum in it, and the picturesque bungalows along St. Martin's looked stark in the gray, pre-storm light. LaForge sped past them up to Paradrome and the Jaguar made a little whine as he down-shifted at the corner and turned left on Ida.

Most of Mt. Adams is too trendy for my taste, too expensive to enjoy and too characterless and chameleon-like to fall in love with. But Ida Street . . . that's my exception. Built on an arched viaduct above a green grove of flowering apple trees, it runs like a bright ribbon between the Art Museum and the East Bottoms. And, for a block or two beyond Seasongood Pavillion, it is as attractive as a crowded urban street can be. The houses along that stretch are those rarities of big city architecture—homes that the architects have built to please themselves. Each of them is unique, in this city of red-brick St. Louises and ranch-style suburbs. Each one of them is full of character and thought and good, adventuresome taste.

LaForge pulled up abruptly in front of one of my favorites—a lovely white stucco building, vaguely Spanish in style, with two Chinese red doors in front and tall blinded windows between them. I watched him unlock the right-hand door with his own key and flash a puckish grin at someone standing inside.

I pulled a pair of Leitz binoculars out of the glove compartment and took a look at the door. The placard by the bell said, "Tracy Leach," which could be a man or woman. From the way Preston had been dressed, I guessed a lady. And it was obvious that Tracy Leach was a very close friend.

I liked the fact that he'd gone to a friend to talk things out. It meant that Preston wasn't as impulsive as he'd seemed, that he had an adult sense of the precariousness of his position.

It was best, I decided, to leave him to his own counsel. If I stuck my nose in again, I might frighten him into running to the Jellicoes or to the police. And I didn't want that to happen until I had Cindy Ann Evans back. Or, at least, until I knew where her bones were resting. A thin splatter of rain dashed the windshield as I turned the ignition key. And it continued to drizzle all the way back to the Delores.

When I got upstairs—fourth floor, right wing, Apartment E-1 stripped off my sports shirt, sat down on the recliner and pretended to read the sports page of *The Enquirer*. But the langorous smell of perfume and the slightly sugary smell of face powder—Jo's scent—distracted me. I kept seeing her in my mind's eye, standing in the hall that led to the bedroom or by the pointed arch that opened on the kitchenette or by the front door. What I was doing was moving her around, mentally, as if she were a piece of outsized furniture and I was trying to fit her in the room. But she was just too large for the two and one-half shabby rooms of the Delores. I started thinking that maybe I'd have to move to a place spacious enough for the two of us. And for the next half hour I settled into a quaint domestic mode of speculation—outfitting the new place, imagining Jo and me in bed, naming the kids. Which only goes to prove my theory that a thirty-six-year-old bachelor is just a thirty-six-year-old husband without a marriage license.

At ten of six, the old Delores rocked like a boat when the sky finally opened up and bellowed, "Enough!" Thick rain, thunderclaps, and lightening poured down on Cincinnati; and I spent a couple of minutes closing windows, a couple more looking out on the waving branches of the dogwoods in the front yard and wondering if Jo was getting drenched. It was going to be a long, sore, wet night

—a real mid-summer deluge. And I didn't look forward to driving back up to Mt. Adams in the midst of it.

By a quarter past, I was beginning to worry about Jo and about why Preston was taking so long with the Jellicoes and with Cindy Ann. My first problem was solved almost immediately, when Jo, black hair collapsed about her face and neat secretary's suit sopping, came laughing and shaking and dripping through the front door.

"My God," she said merrily. "It could have waited a few minutes longer!"

I jumped up and gave her a hug and a long, damp kiss. She was as slippery as soap in her wet skin, but otherwise no worse for the weather. She wandered off into the bedroom to towel dry and change clothes, and I sat back down, feeling aglow, and stared at the phone on the desk. By all dramatic rights, it, too, was about to ring and Preston would then say, in his cheeky, affable voice, "I've got Cindy Ann for you." And then we'd all join hands and form a ring.

But Preston didn't call until after Jo and I had dined on scrambled eggs and on each other. We were lying in the bed, holding hands and listening like nervous children with the lights out to the beating of the rain on the dormer window and the tremendous claps of thunder when the phone rang.

I'd told Jo a little bit about Preston while we were eating supper. I'm not usually a gossip about my work, but LaForge was too juicy and out-of-the-ordinary for me. And I'd told her about Hugo, whom she'd already met and liked and felt sorry for. That seedy old man had a way with women. Jo'd thought he was "sweet" and wanted to see him again. I hadn't said a thing about the Jellicoes, because I hadn't wanted to spoil our lovemaking with the thought of how they made their living. Jo knew that Hugo's "little girl" was in trouble and that La-Forge was somehow involved and that he was an odd fellow who was going to help me crack the case.

Anyway, when the phone rang, she giggled and said, "That must be him!"

I reached over and pulled the phone down to the bed and, with Jo cocking an ear against the receiver, said, "Stoner."

Either the telephone lines were damp or Preston was drunk, because his voice sounded scratchy and lethargic. "I did what you said, Mr. Stoner," he said. "I got it all arranged. I've been a good boy."

Jo looked at me and I looked at her and shrugged.

"That's good, Preston. That's very good."

"You know," he said languidly. "In a way I'm glad this is going to work out this way. I'm really tired of the whole thing. After this, I'm going to be good. You'll see."

I felt a little heartsick, and Jo stopped listening and stared at the ceiling. "You don't have to be good, Preston," I said, trying to sound friendly. "Maybe if you stopped thinking about yourself in those terms you'd be better off."

He laughed, his little boy's chortle. "You sound like Dr. Fegley."

"Well, maybe Dr. Fegley knows what he's talking about."

"He doesn't know," Preston said blandly. "Nobody does."

I took a deep breath and changed the subject. "What time should I come by tonight?"

"What?" he said. "Oh. About ten, I guess. That's when they usually drop the girls off. Lance is going to call me in an hour or so to let me know for sure. Boy, I really shook him up, Mr. Stoner. I really gave it to him. He's not going to use me anymore. Not me or any of my friends."

A very ugly thought crossed my mind. "You didn't threaten him, did you, Preston? I mean you didn't tell him you'd gone to the cops or anything, did you?"

"I did what I had to do," he said. "I should have done it a long time ago."

I started to say something cautionary and Preston said, "Don't worry about Cindy Ann, Mr. Stoner. He says he won't hurt her as long as the cops aren't called in. And he won't hurt me, either. Tray and I know too much. I'll tell you this, though. As soon as you get Cindy Ann back to her folks, I *am* going to go to the police and tell them everything I know about the Jellicoes. I want to. I've wanted to for years. I'm not a very courageous man, Mr. Stoner. I never have been." He laughed unhappily. "Now, I won't have to pretend any more."

I blew a cold breath out of my mouth. "What makes you think he'll show up with Cindy Ann?"

"Like I said, Mr. Stoner. All Lance cares about is the police. I gave him my word they weren't involved."

"You've done well, Preston," I said to him. "You're a good man."

"Thanks," he said. "I'll see you tonight at ten."

When I hung up, Jo was lying on her side with her shoulder to me. Something about the curve of that shoulder told me that she didn't want to be touched. At least, not by me. Not at that moment. And, to tell you the truth, at that moment I couldn't blame her.

═══════

The rest of the evening didn't go well for Jo and me. The scarey, shivery storm became just a storm. The bedside lamps dispelled the sweet privacy of the darkness. We sat in bed and read—Mary Ellmann for her, Dashiell Hammett for me—and chatted occasionally and pointed out fun things in what we were reading and pretended that nothing had gone wrong.

I should never have said a word about the case is what I thought. I should have buttoned my lip and kept mum about Preston LaForge, the all-American boy.

Around nine I got up, got dressed and drank a cup of coffee in the living room. Jo came in and asked if I was going out in the storm.

I nodded.

She looked at me affectionately and said, "I guess I must have thought of Preston LaForge as one of the immortals. To find out he was *so* damn human . . . it just upset me. Don't mind me, Harry. You broke one of my idols, that's all."

"He was one of my idols, too, Jo," I said testily. "And I didn't break him. He broke. You don't think a man spills his guts like that because another man flashes a few dirty pictures in his face? Preston La-Forge has been breaking down since he was an adolescent. And if he hasn't made good resolutions a thousand times before—and then forgotten them—I'll eat the radio."

"You're probably right," she said. "You know detectives aren't ordinary mortals either. At least, they haven't been in my life."

She smiled and said, "Give me a few days to adjust."

Jo sat down on the couch beside me and stared out the rainy window. "It's nasty out there. Will you be gone long?"

"I don't know," I said. "Maybe an hour or two."

"You're still angry, aren't you?"

I was, though I pretended not to be. She wasn't the real reason I was angry, anyway. I was worried about what was waiting for me on Celestial. I could show up and find Lance Jellicoe sitting on the stoop. It wasn't all that likely, not if Preston hadn't done something foolish like waving the Vice Squad at the Jellicoes. But the melancholy bravado in his voice had made me nervous. While Jo was in the kitchenette, I went over to the desk and got a .38 caliber Police Special out of the right-hand drawer. I slipped it in my coat pocket and pulled a hat from the rack.

"Wait!" Jo shouted.

She came running up to me at the door and kissed me hard on the mouth.

I laughed. "The iconoclast's farewell?"

"Just be careful, Harry. *Please*. I don't care about broken idols. I just want you to come back in one piece."

———

It was, indeed, a very nasty night out there.

The wind was shaking the dogwoods as I walked out the front door, and the footpath that led to the rear lot was slick with waxy leaves. I was soaked to the skin before I got to the Pinto.

It took me twenty minutes to get to Mt. Adams and another five to wind my way around the crabbed streets to Celestial and the Vicarage.

The courtyard was bright and wet and full of rain and of the sound the rain made as it exploded against the cobbling. Most of the light was coming from the rear windows of the five or six condos that faced away from the river and toward Hyde Park. There were dark figures in some of those yellow windows, but the wind-blown rain was smeared like jam on the glass. I couldn't tell a man from a woman, much less make out a face.

I cracked the car door open and made a quick dash to the sweet-smelling cedar tunnel that led to LaForge's apartment. The rain made a drum-like sound inside the tunnel, which was lit brightly by a series of lanterns strung along the west wall. I wiped the water off my face and shook my sleeve out and started down the walkway and, right away, I could see that something was very wrong.

There were two condos on the west side of the tunnel. The one at the rear was LaForge's, and its door was wide open and banging in the wind. I shivered through my wet coat and pulled the revolver out of my pocket and edged down the hall to the open door.

There were no lights on inside the LaForge apartment, but as I neared the door I could hear a woman's recorded voice singing softly. I ducked down beside the frame. If there was someone inside waiting, I would make a perfect target coming through the door. For at least a second, I'd be framed like a picture and illuminated by the light from the small lantern hanging on the outer wall. I stood up, back pressed against the redwood, and, reaching to my right, cracked a pane of the lantern with the gun butt. The glass made a bright tinkling sound as it hit the walkway and the last third of the tunnel went dark.

I ducked back down immediately and, pressing an arm against my torso to reduce the size of the target I'd make, I swung around the door frame, rolled onto the cream-colored carpet and flattened myself against the floor.

There wasn't a sound inside but the sweet singing voice from the record, which I now recognized as Barbra Streisand's voice. The rain was cascading down the great triangular window across the room from me, but some diffuse light was filtering through from neighboring condos. As my eyes adjusted to it, I made out Preston LaForge lying in the center of the room beneath the cathedral-like vault of the ceiling. Something about the stillness of that body sent a thrill of horror down my spine. I crept about five feet into the room and listened for the sounds of breathing or of movement.

There wasn't any sound but the rain. And, as my heart beat slowed down and the hair-raising prickle of adrenaline washed out of my system, I realized that there probably *wasn't* going to be any sound but the rain. Not with that body lying in the center of the room and the front door wide open. Whoever had been there before me had left in a rush. Either appalled by what was lying on the floor or frightened away from what he or she had done. On the surface, it didn't look like a murder or, if it had been, it was a pretty sloppy one, executed on the spur of the moment. High class killers rarely leave doors open or track up cream-colored rugs. There was muddy scuffing on the floor, just visible in the thin greenish light.

I didn't want to do it, but it had to be done. And quickly, if I was to get out of that building without being spotted. And God knew, I didn't want to be spotted. Not with a gun in my pocket and a dead body in the room and a snapshot floating around somewhere which could be traced back to me. I pocketed the revolver and walked quickly over to the window and examined Preston LaForge for any sign of life. The rain-filtered light streaked his face, making it look like something seen through the glass of an aquarium. One side of it looked as boyish as it had when I'd seen him that afternoon. The blue eye was open and placid. The other side had no eye and no shape and I didn't look at it long. His babyish mouth had fallen open in an aghast grin and a thick smear of blood covered the chin and flowed down the neck and pooled in a shiny spot on the rug.

That was one stain he wasn't going to get out. Ever. The poor, sad, son-of-a-bitch.

I took a long look at the body, trying to fix it and everything around it in my mind. A small caliber automatic was lying near LaForge's hand. There were foot-tracks beside his left shoulder and throughout the room. The record was playing "Until the Right Man Comes Along." There were no lit cigarettes in ashtrays. There was a whiskey glass on the glass coffee table in front of the couch. There was something else on the coffee table. Something white.

A tremendous crack of thunder made me jump, and I almost stepped in the pool of Preston La-Forge's blood. I walked quickly to the coffee table and pulled a damp handkerchief from my pocket. And used it to pick up the piece of paper sitting on the table. There was a name written on it and a phone number. It said "Tracy" and underneath the name was written "899-7010." I dropped the slip of paper back on the coffee table and repeated the phone number as I walked back to the door.

It's best to do these things boldly, I told myself. A ridiculous thing to say, since "these things" happen once in a lifetime. But it gave me a vague sense of confidence.

I stepped out into the tunnel and just kept walking briskly across the courtyard to the Pinto. I didn't look up or right or left. If anyone could see me through the rain, it wouldn't do me a damn bit of good if I saw him, too. I got in the car and pulled out and didn't turn on any lights until I was well onto Celestial with the Vicarage a block behind me.

# 14

**"IT SHOULDN'T HAVE** happened this way."

That was the first thing I told myself, when I felt like I could talk again without my throat backing up.

I was sitting in the car on the Ida Street viaduct across from Tracy Leach's white stucco dream house. And I'd been sitting there for ten minutes—smoking Chesterfields, drinking from a flask I keep in the glove compartment, and trying to calm down.

"It shouldn't have happened this way," I said again. "No one should have been hurt."

It was logic meant for a dead man with a broken face, who wasn't going to be convinced by the argument or appeased by the tone of apology, and it made me feel sick and sad all over again to say it. I stared out at the rain from the seat of the Pinto and felt bad for Preston LaForge.

Yet, I knew I had to be right, that it *shouldn't*

have happened, that LaForge *shouldn't* have been dead, and that that damn girl should have been sitting on the car seat next to me. But that's the trouble with the subjunctive mood; it's always one tempo ahead of or behind the inexorable, should-less flow of events.

"I should have had her!" I said aloud. But she wouldn't be convinced either. And it was just more bad philosophy to blame her or Hugo for what had happened. They weren't responsible. I wasn't sure who was.

People killed themselves every day. Even people with as much to live for as Preston LaForge. And it was barely possible that his death didn't have anything to do with me or the girl or the Jellicoes. Barely possible. But not likely. What was likely was that a plan which should have worked with minimal risk had ended in death. And it had been my plan; so, to the degree that I'd fobbed it off on Preston LaForge, I was feeling responsible.

It wasn't as if he'd gone into the whole thing blindfolded, with me prodding him with a gun in his back. I knew for a fact that he had weighed the risks. And in good company, too. Tracy Leach, Preston's "Tray," was not the innocent girlfriend I had pictured earlier that afternoon. Judging from what LaForge had said over the phone, she was as familiar with the Jellicoes' operation as Preston had been. And, therefore, should have been qualified to judge how far Lance and Laurie could be pushed before it came to shove. She'd apparently approved La-

Forge's strategy late that day, when he'd come visiting in his Ralph Lauren outfit. Which meant that something that neither she nor Preston had anticipated had gone wrong enough to drive Preston to suicide or to drive the Jellicoes to murder him. And it was that something that made me breathe more easily, because it was that something that I could never have foretold. Whatever it was, it was somehow connected to a red-haired sixteen-year-old girl with a thin, avaricious face and a market value that seemed to keep soaring far beyond any reasonable estimate. Whatever it was, it was unpredictable and fatal. And, in the rain and the dark, Tracy Leach had seemed like one of the few people who might be able to guess.

At ten-thirty, I got out of the car and dashed through the storm to the Chinese-red door of the Leach house. Lights were on on the first floor, but no one answered my knock. I tried the doorbell, knocked again, and suddenly realized that Tray wasn't going to answer no matter how many times I banged at the door. In a bizarre way, Preston La-Forge had told me why.

He wouldn't have needed to write down her phone number. Not if he had a key to the house. Which meant that Tracy Leach was out for the evening and that the number I'd memorized belonged to the home she was visiting.

Deep down I was glad she wasn't home. Glad because I didn't want to break the news to her. Glad because I didn't want to press her into service, at least not on that unlucky night. Glad because if she wouldn't cooperate, if Preston's death didn't shake her into action, I'd have to try the same ploy on her that I'd used on LaForge. Tell her that I knew that same dirty, ruinous secret and that I'd tell the world if she wouldn't play along.

Hugo or no Hugo, Cindy Ann simply wasn't worth it. Not to me. Not on that night.

———

Jo looked shaken when I unlocked the front door of my apartment. She'd been sitting by the phone in front of the rolltop desk and, when I trudged through the door, she jumped to her feet and threw her arms around me.

"You'll get wet," I said softly.

She held me at arm's length and looked me over. "Thank God, you're all right. You *are* all right, aren't you?"

I shook the hat off and pegged it on the rack and said, "I guess I am," without much conviction.

"I heard it on the radio about an hour after you left. A neighbor found him in the living room. I couldn't believe it! Preston LaForge!" She pulled me against her. "Then I got that damn phone call and I didn't know what—"

"What phone call?"

She pointed to a yellow tablet on the desk. "I wrote it down for you. He said you should call him tonight."

I walked over to the rolltop and read what was

written on the tablet. "Lance Jellicoe called," it said. "At 10:30. *Has* to talk with you about tonight."

"That man had a brutal voice," Jo said nervously.

"He's a very brutal man," I told her.

"Then why . . ."

Jo looked at me haplessly. She was being better than considerate. She was being *good*, in the reformed, touching way that children are good after an argument or an ugly scene. It moved me enough to want to tell her everything she was dying to know. And I told her that I would, as I picked up the phone and dialed Jellicoe's number.

Jellicoe answered on the fifth ring in a grumpy, inhospitable voice. He sounded edgy and just the slightest bit confused, as if he weren't quite sure he wanted to talk with anyone. I could understand that, especially if he thought the police might be calling.

"This is Stoner," I said to him.

His voice toughened a little. "You go by LaForge's apartment?"

"Yeah."

"Then you seen what happened to him. Before you call the police, I want you to know that Laurie and me had nothing to do with that. You hear? Nothing. Don't make no difference if you believe me. Truth is I like Preston. He was a good ol' boy. He had his faults, but meanness wasn't one of them."

Once he'd gotten that out of the way, Jellicoe got down to business.

"Now, you listen to me, mister," he said. "You want that girl back, you won't tell the police about us. Hear? We'll lose her sure as hell if you do."

"Why didn't you deliver her to LaForge?" I said to him. "Why did he kill himself?"

"I don't know about that," Lance said with a surprising depth of feeling. "He was dead when we got over there. Don't make much sense to me. A man like him. Don't make no sense a'tall."

I didn't believe Lance Jellicoe. At least, I didn't think I did. But I found that I had to remind myself that he was certainly a pimp and possibly a killer—his tone was that far removed from what I'd anticipated.

"Where's the girl?" I said.

"We'll get to that." And suddenly his tone wasn't odd at all. "You meet Laurie tomorrow night. Bring one of them pictures with you. She'll tell you about Cindy Ann."

I thought it over quickly. I didn't understand the importance of the pictures, although it was clear enough why the Jellicoes wanted the police kept out of their affairs. "I'll come," I told him. "But on my terms. We meet where I say and when I say. And if there's any trouble, Lance, the pictures and a deposition get sent straight to the cops."

"Call it," he said.

"The Busy Bee. At six tomorrow night."

"She'll be there," he said and hung up.

I put the phone back in its cradle and stared at the desk top. If I'd have been the head-scratching, chin-pulling type, I would have been paring away at my sandy noggin and my chin would have been stretched out like taffy. It just didn't make any sense. Jellicoe calling me up, suddenly showing interest in those snapshots, practically agreeing to be blackmailed. He must have found out about me and my little photo album through Preston or Abel Jones. That was clear cut. What I couldn't understand was why the hell he'd be so interested in a scummy picture that no one could trace back to him or to his organization. I thought about it until it became obvious. And then I laughed out loud—a single bark of berserk amusement. It wasn't at all funny. If I'd thought of it a few hours earlier in the day, Preston LaForge might still be alive.

"What's wrong?" Jo said uncertainly.

"He thinks he's in those pictures!" I said, half to myself.

"What pictures?"

I looked at her a second. She cocked her head and looked back at me expectantly. She had every right to know, and I had every reason not to tell her.

"Are you sure you want to hear this?" I said.

She nodded. "I think I have the right to know."

"I guess you do, too." I opened the lower right-hand drawer of the desk and took out the box of photographs. "These are pictures of Cindy Ann Evans. Hugo's Cindy Ann. They were taken by the Jellicoes." I patted the lid and handed the box to Jo. "Now you'll understand why the old man wants her back."

I talked to her as she sorted through the photos, not looking at her because I knew what her reaction would be. Disgust, horror, anger—the same responses I had had. Besides, I needed to talk about the Jellicoes. I needed to air my own ideas, and I needed someone to hear them, to make them seem real or, at least, plausible.

"I think the Jellicoes want those pictures because they think they might be in some of them. They're not sure, though. And that's what interests me. Having been photographed with Cindy Ann Evans must be a powerful liability. Or else Lance Jellicoe would never have risked calling me and blowing his alibi by telling me he was at the LaForge apartment tonight."

I looked over at Jo. Her hands were folded on the shoe box and she was staring at them as if they were pictures of her hands taken in an untroubled year.

"You don't want to hear this, do you?" I said gently.

"Why not?" she said in a dull, wounded voice. "I don't think anything you could tell me could be worse than what I just saw."

"I warned you."

She shuddered and said, "Not strongly enough." Jo looked up from her hands. "What's happened to the little girl, Harry? Do you know?"

"This afternoon, I wasn't sure. Now . . ."

I took a breath and said, "I think she's dead, Jo."

I'd said it for myself, as well as for her, to take the sting out of it by making it conscious. But all it did for me was remind me of Hugo and of the dreadful look on LaForge's face. And, as for Jo, she looked back down at her hands and started to cry. "My God, what an awful thing. Why would they do it? She's just a child."

I sat back heavily in the chair. I was sorry I had told her. I was sorry I'd admitted it to myself. "I don't know why. All I know is that the Jellicoes don't want any photographs lying around that could connect them with Cindy Ann Evans. And, to me, that means that Cindy Ann Evans is in serious trouble. I could be wrong. But she did drop out of sight. And LaForge is dead, maybe by his own hand, as a result of something that I started this afternoon by showing him those same pictures."

"It's not your fault," Jo said hoarsely. She wiped her eyes with her fingertips and asked, "What did he have to do with the girl anyway?"

I wasn't going to make the same mistake twice. Not with Jo feeling so vulnerable. And not with LaForge newly dead. I owed him something for trying to be a good boy, and the bitterest part of the truth didn't seem like too much to pay.

"Nothing," I told her. "He was just an acquaintance of the Jellicoes. He was just a means of getting in touch with them. Preston was an unhappy man who couldn't live up to his all-American image. And

I just happened to catch up with him on the last day of his life."

"Bad luck," Jo said, closing off the topic.

She got up from her chair and walked slowly toward the bedroom. "Bad luck for you both."

# 15

MONDAY STARTED OFF as badly as Sunday had ended. Hugo called at half-past eight, and I spent half an hour trying to convince him that everything was fine and that he should stay with his son in Dayton. It's hard to lie convincingly very early or very late in the day—salesmen and bill collectors know it and so, I think, did Hugo Cratz. Try as I might to make my sleepy voice sound cheerful and confident, some of the previous night—some of that horror that Jo had written off as bad luck—seeped in. And Hugo caught it, the way a dog catches a trace of dogginess in an old rug.

"Hold up, now, Harry," he said crankily. "Just what's going on down there? I got the right to know."

They were Jo's very words and, like Jo, he'd spoken the truth. He *did* have the right to know. But, after what had happened the night before, I just wasn't prepared to tell him. So I tried to edge around the ugly part and, at the same time, to suggest what had occurred to me as soon as I saw Preston LaForge's shattered face. "Right now, I'm not having much luck finding her, Hugo. I'm beginning to think that it wouldn't be a bad idea to let the police in on it."

"Police!" he exploded. "Damn it, I told you I didn't want no cops sniffing around my little girl. If you're getting tired of helping me, just let me know. I got other places I can go."

Like where? I almost said.

And I almost said, "What if she's dead." But it would be a hellish mistake if I were wrong. So there was nothing to do but tell him, "I'll keep at it," and to mumble a silent prayer that the Jellicoes could be bluffed into telling me what had become of Cindy Ann.

Only that seemed more and more unlikely as the day started in earnest over coffee and the newspaper and the sounds of Jo showering and getting dressed. The Jellicoes had no intention of trading information to me. Moreover, I had nothing to trade. Once Laurie saw one of the pictures and realized that neither she nor Lance was in it, I'd be cooked. That is, unless I could convince her that the photos were more damaging than they seemed, unless I could keep her guessing about what they really pictured. It would be a risky bluff. Perhaps a fatal one, if Jellicoe had been lying to me about LaForge's death, if, in fact, he were setting me up the way I had set up Preston. What it came down to was the tricky question of how far the Jellicoes could be pushed. And, at ten in the morning, the only person I could think of who might know was Tracy Leach—the woman I'd sworn to leave alone the night before.

It's always depressing to recognize just how fragile good intentions are. Preston's, my own, and Jo's. That "bad luck" business wasn't going to carry her through the day, and she was seething as she walked into the living room. She sat down on the couch and I passed her a cup of coffee and the morning *Enquirer*. As soon as she saw the front page, the big picture of Preston and the smarmy headline, it all came out in one confused burst.

"You got a lousy job, Harry!" she muttered. "And I hate it. I hate what I saw last night. And I hate the people you deal with. And right now, I hate you for being part of the whole thing!"

She shot up from the couch and I grabbed her hand. "It's not that I'm a coward," she said. "You know I'm not. I've seen terrible things in my life. And I've survived them. I'll survive this, too. The thing is I just don't know whether I want to commit myself to a relationship with a man whose professional life is like the buried half of a log. I don't need any more grief. I want something . . ." Her gray eyes darted about the room as if the word she were looking for were hidden in a corner. "Quieter."

She pulled away and said, "I'm going to go home now and think about this."

She started for the door and whirled around and pointed an accusatory finger at me. "I think I could love you, damn it! I think I already do. And what I want to know is what you're going to do about it."

"I love you, too," I said helplessly, which, I suppose, is the only way it's ever said.

"Well, goddamn it!" Jo said and stalked out of the room. "I'll be at the Bee tonight," she called over her shoulder. "I'm off at ten."

———

I'd dressed in a pair of light gray slacks and a pale blue broadcloth shirt, and I'd dug through the closet until I found a navy blazer that didn't look as if it had been torn from the rack during a twelve-hour sale. I wanted to look natty and reputable for Miss Tracy Leach and, standing in the bright morning sunlight in front of her jewel-like house and watching the sparse traffic saunter down Ida Street, I felt relatively respectable.

I'd tried to picture what she'd look like as I'd driven over to Mt. Adams. But what does a rich, young woman with a jaded sexual palate and Preston LaForge for a boyfriend look like? She could be anything from a robust and rambunctious Dallas Cowgirl to one of those ethereal young things with blue-veined, china-white skin and large nervous eyes. All I knew for certain was that she liked her callers well-dressed.

Looking up at that exquisite house with its Chinese red doors, I decided that she was probably closer to the ethereal type—one of those shy, serious, half-pretty young women who prefer the company of weak and troubled men. The kind who has hundreds of "friends" in different places and who lives nervously from friend to friend in an endless round of homing and small talk and idle, uneventful romance. She was probably thin and blonde and gauzy-looking. And she would dress elegantly and speak in a soft, shy shimmer, like the slip of a small blue wave. I liked the woman I had conjured up on the doorstep and decided to handle her with care.

I knocked once at the red door.

A pale, straw-haired man—shirtless beneath a white waiter's jacket and navy-blue pin-striped pants—answered it. In the face, he had the fragile look of the young Truman Capote; but, as with those photographs of the young Capote, there was a distant malice in his pale green eyes and something absolutely vicious about the cut of his mouth, which was much redder than the rest of his face and seemed to stand out from the surrounding flesh as if it were carved in bas-relief. Beneath that face, he was wiry and slender. But not at all weak-looking. Twin cords of muscle pillared his neck, and his pale naked chest had the oiled, overdeveloped musculature of the weight-lifter. He was about forty years old and wore that boyish face as if he were thoroughly tired of being told how young it looked.

"Yes?" he said. "What is it?"

"I want to speak with Tracy," I said. "Is she home?"

The man grinned nastily. It made him look his forty years and then some. "Is this a joke?" he said and I could see the muscles beneath that waiter's jacket tightening up. "Because if it is, I don't think it's funny." His face fell suddenly and for a second I thought he was going to cry. "I've had an awful night and if Tony or Mark or one of that crowd sent you over here to rag me, I'm warning you now I'm in no mood for games. Maybe they didn't tell you, but I'm expert at sabot. And I can assure you that if you don't get off this porch in two seconds, I'm going to give you a lesson that you'll never forget."

I stepped back from the door and looked down at myself ruefully, at those clothes I had hand-picked for Miss Tracy Leach. I wanted to laugh, but I knew that if I did he'd start kicking. It was an awful joke, anyway. And if I hadn't been such a sentimentalist, I would have seen it coming sooner. Serves you right, I told myself, for making the world over in your own image.

"Uh . . . *you're* Tracy Leach," I said. "Aren't you?"

He nodded.

"I'm sorry about the mistake in gender, Mr. Leach. No joke was intended. I was under the impression that Tray was a girl."

"Tray!" he said and squinted at me. "Do I know you?"

"No. But I knew Preston LaForge and he mentioned your name to me."

Leach winced at Preston's name and gripped his

belly. "You're the detective!" he said in a painted, aghast voice. "You're the one who got him killed!"

Leach bent forward and straightened suddenly, as if something had locked inside his spine. He let out a blood-curdling yell and sent his left, shoeless foot flying toward my head.

He shouldn't have yelled. They say that's supposed to freeze your target, but it only made me jump. The foot whistled by my temple and I went charging forward, knocking him off his right leg and back into the house.

He went down on his butt and I pinned him with my body, but not very successfully. He just kept yelling and kicking and throwing his head around like a frenzied child. Some of those kicks were finding their mark on my ankles and on my legs and dangerously close to my knees.

"Cut it out!" I shouted at him.

When he didn't stop, I clipped him hard—a foreshortened right cross that landed on the tip of his chin.

His body went limp and his head lolled to the carpet.

"Jesus Christ!" I said as I got to my feet.

I rubbed my sore legs and took a quick look at Tray. He wasn't going to start kicking again for a few minutes at least, which gave me a moment or so to examine the room. It was a rose-colored parlor, an old-fashioned sitting room, furnished predictably with Chinese screens and Beardsley prints and velvet Victorian settees with inlaid burl and carved oriental teak boxes with brass handles and an oversized rosewood chiffonier filled with expensive knick-nacks. It was a rich, eccentric old woman's room—many homosexuals have a dowager's taste in fur-nishings, but flashier, like the old woman discovered sex at the age of seventy. It depressed me. Tracy Leach depressed me. And so did Preston LaForge. The all-American boy.

It didn't look like Tray was going to come out of it on his own, so I grabbed him by the collar of his waiter's jacket and dragged him over to one of those squat Chinese boxes. There was a silver bowl on top of it, filled with water and floated with rose petals. I dumped the whole thing on Leach's head and stepped back.

He sputtered and shook and wiped the petals off his face.

Leach sat up when he'd gotten his bearings and looked in horror at the rug. "These things are ex-pensive," he blubbered. "Who's going to pay to have this cleaned?" He got slowly to his feet and stared at the waterspot on the carpet.

"Why don't you have Oscar come in and redecorate?" I said drily.

Leach looked at me with surprise. "You know Oscar?"

I laughed in spite of myself.

"There's nothing funny about this." Leach kneeled down and prodded the carpet.

For a split second I had the feeling he was about

to attack me again. So I said to him, "Don't try it, Tracy."

"Bully," he said, straightening up.

I folded my arms and shook my head at him. "That's always the way it is with you guys, isn't it? The world's always divided into two camps—the bullies and the gays."

"That happens to be the way it is."

"Don't make me sick, Tray," I said. "I know too much about you to fall for that put-upon crap. You buy little boys and girls. Just like Preston did. You probably shared a few with him, calling him up like a housewife passing along a good recipe. So don't get self-righteous with me."

Tracy Leach squeezed a little rose-water out of his sleeves and walked over to one of the velvet settees. "What do you want from me?" he said.

"Some information about the Jellicoes."

He sat down delicately on the edge of a cushion and looked disbelievingly into my face. "You must think I'm crazy. You saw what happened to Pres. Why in God's name do you think I would try the same thing?"

I shrugged. "I thought maybe you'd want to do something for a dead friend."

"Like what?" he said viciously.

"Like finding out who killed him."

"He killed himself," Leach said. "Preston would have killed himself some day no matter what I or anyone else did." He took a husky, sorrowful breath and sat up on the settee. "He just couldn't handle

**167**

being gay. He'd do stupid, dangerous things. Make jokes, expose himself publicly. All he ever really wanted was to be caught and . . . sent home." Leach massaged his face as if it were a knotted muscle. "I'm not like Preston, Mr.—"

"Stoner."

"Stoner. I made my choice, if you can call it that, early in life. And most of the time, I'm not ashamed of it or disturbed by it. You asked me before how deep my loyalties went. Well, you won't understand it, but I loved Preston and I tried to protect him while he was alive. Now . . ." Leach dropped his hands to the settee.

I studied him for a second. Muscling the poor bastard wasn't going to help Cindy Ann Evans. I reached into my pocket and pulled out a card and set it on the Chinese box. "All right, Tray. Call me if you change your mind."

"I won't, you know," he said. "I don't know why I should say this. I don't like you. And I don't approve of what you did to Preston. But, if you're smart, you'll leave this alone. They're a ruthless pair. And if you keep investigating this girl's disappearance, they will kill you.

"Now get out," he said. "Get out and leave me alone."

I walked through the front door into the bright July sun and tried to think of one good reason why I shouldn't find another line of work.

# 16

I WAS OUT along the river in half an hour, coasting past the barren industrial landscape of Riverview—past the big oil depots and the railroad yards, where the track smiled savagely in the noon sun. And then the tanks and the tank cars vanished, and I could see the river again, the somber brown Ohio, as it jaunted southwest down the roller-coaster slope of the Kentucky line.

Five more miles due west and I came to the lonely frame house on the clay flats. I pulled over to the embankment, cut the engine and just sat, for a moment, on the seat—smelling the river again as it was borne in across the desolate yard and up the marl slope. But this time it didn't carry the jungle smells with it—the rot and the diesel oil and the burnt-grass smell of the LZs. This time, the smells were like the fulsome smells of Tray Leach's Spanish house and of the missing girl herself. The smells of a sweet and secret decay, half-hidden, half-wanting to be found. And for more than a moment, I considered nakedly what *I* was really trying to find. A corpse, lying like the black, charred tire in the yard of Abel Jones's house? A killer? A conspiracy? But that wasn't it. The little man knew better, especially after learning what he had about Leach and Preston LaForge. He wanted the source. He wanted Nick himself by the nose.

Suddenly, I was for it, again. For what I couldn't explain to Jo. For what I can't even explain to myself. For finding all secret, evil things and making them known.

A shirtless man had come out on the porch of Jones's house and, with one hand shading his eyes, was gazing up at the Pinto. Even from a hundred yards away I could tell that he wasn't Jones. His hair was too light and too long and his skin had been burned to the color of a mahogany door by the sun. He stared at me for a minute and then started up the slope, moving with great, bearlike swipes of his arms. I got out of the Pinto when he was about twenty-five feet away and leaned against the door handle with one hand holding the pistol in my coat pocket. I wasn't going to have any trouble asking questions of this one—he'd do all the talking, at least at first. It was what happened after he finished that had me a little worried. He was a big strapping kid, and the closer he got the fiercer he looked.

"What is it you're looking for?" he said when he

got up to me. He was older than I thought. Maybe thirty. Brown-haired, high-cheeked, with a touch of Indian blood in his swarthy face.

"I'm looking for Coral Jones," I said to him. "She knows who I am."

"*I* don't," he said plainly. "Maybe you better tell me what your business is."

"My name's Stoner. Coral is helping me find a missing girl."

"Shoot, you'd better find *him* first," the man said.

"Abel?"

"Yeah."

"He's gone?" I said.

"All weekend."

"And Coral?"

He colored a little on his high cheeks. Just enough to give me the feeling that he wasn't sure how to answer the question. Or, perhaps, how Coral would want him to answer it.

"Maybe you'd better talk to the lady," he said at last.

Down we went into the yard, where the Falcon sat next to the frame porch. Then up onto the porch and into the hallway.

There had been a few changes since the last time I'd been there. Most of the portable items—the fairground mementos—had been packed away in liquor boxes, half a dozen of which were stacked on the living room floor. The larger furniture had been covered with throws.

Coral Jones, her head wrapped in a plaid scarf,

was bending over one of the boxes when I walked into the room. She was wearing tight blue jeans and a man's workshirt, which she'd knotted at her waist instead of tucking into the jeans. She smiled, a friendly smile, when she saw me and said to the shirtless man, "Bobby, go out for awhile."

"You sure, Coral?" he said, warning her with his eyes that I was trouble.

"I'm sure, honey. You go on."

He let out a steamy breath, looked bothered and, then, walked out the front door. "I won't be far off," he called over his shoulder.

"Isn't he the sweetest," Coral said with a giggle.

"Where'd you find him?" I said.

"Well, I got to thinking after you left how little I was looking forward to Abel poking me in the eye. And I said to myself, 'Girl, you don't have to take that, either.' So, when he got sober, I just told him we were quits. He took it better than I thought he would. Or worse. I guess it depends on your point of view. Anyway, he left more than two days ago and I haven't seen him since."

Coral patted one of the boxes. "I'm moving away," she said brightly. "Going to make a fresh start, like I told you. That's how I met Bobby. He's helping me move out. He's a nice-looking boy, isn't he?" She peeked out the front door to where Bobby was marching back and forth in the yard. "A little young," she said with a blush. "But he's sure enough willing."

"I'll bet."

Coral laughed. "I guess I owe all of this to you, in a way. What brings you around here, anyway?"

"I need some help, Coral," I told her. "Things just haven't been falling my way, lately. And I need some help."

"About that girl?" she said.

I nodded.

Coral pointed to the couch and I sat down. "You want a drink? I've got a bottle right over here."

She lifted a half-filled quart of Old Grandad from behind the couch and plucked two glasses out of a crate. "Here," she said, handing me a glass.

She plopped down on the couch beside me and curled up, like a cat making herself comfortable. "So what can I do for you?"

I took a quick look at her—brown and pretty and fairly bursting her shirt and slacks. And she smiled shyly, as if to say that it was all right if that's what I wanted. And, I suppose, a huge disloyal part of me did. But then I thought of Jo and felt properly chastened. Absurd, in this insanely picaresque universe, to obligate yourself to one person, to make up loyalties that time itself, not to mention whim, chance or change of weather, will explode like hurtled glass. Absurd, I told myself. And knew that it was even more absurd to protest. So, I shook my head sadly and balefully and said, "I'm probably crazy, Coral. But what I want from you is some information."

"I'd like to help you if I can."

"Then tell me all you know about Laurie and

Lance Jellicoe. Because things have changed since Friday. A man is dead. That girl may be dead. Both at their hands."

"Could be," Coral said. "Like I told you before, they're a rough pair, although, from what I've seen, murder's not exactly their style."

"What is their style?"

"Blackmail," she said. "Blackmail and raw sex. They've got quite a list of customers, too, from what Abel used to tell me. Abel liked that part best. He liked to see the mighty brought low. Hell, Abel liked to see anyone brought low."

"Do you know any names or places. Customers I might talk to or houses where they might keep their store of little boys and girls?"

Coral shook her head. "For a talkative man, Abel could be mighty close-mouthed when it came to things that really counted."

"Damn it!" I said. "I've got to meet that girl tonight. And I need some kind of edge."

Coral looked about the room as if she were checking to make sure that no one was listening. "You know about Escorts Unlimited, right?"

I nodded. "And the office on Plum Street. And the prostitution in Newport."

She shrugged. "Then I don't know what more I can tell you. Abel was just a part-time handyman for them. I do know that they had him working over in Kentucky. And that sometimes he'd be gone for a couple of days at a time. But, knowing Abel like I do, that could mean any number of things."

I swallowed the rest of the drink and put the glass down on one of the liquor boxes. "Well, I gave it a try anyway. I'll just have to bluff it out with what I've got."

"Hold on a second," Coral said. "Do you know about the other one?"

For a second I didn't know what she was talking about, what that slightly sinister phrase meant. But it chilled me just the same. "What do you mean?"

"The partner," she said, looking anxiously into her drink. "The other one."

"Whoa!" I said and it was as if I'd gotten a second wind on that hot, windless afternoon.

She looked up from her glass and smiled broadly when she'd realized that she'd given me something I could use. "Don't go asking me what his name is. Hell, I don't even know for sure if he's a he! But I do know that someone else works with them. Abel knew his name. And I had the feeling that he was the brains behind the escort service."

"What does he look like, this partner?"

"Oh, Harry," she said, and I thought she would cry. "Honey, I just don't know."

"Do you know why they wanted Abel to get rid of those pictures—like the one of Cindy Ann?"

She bit her lip. "They didn't need those pictures —the ones with just the girls in them. There were others that they'd keep."

"For blackmail?"

She nodded.

"Where did they take these pictures?" I asked her.

"That I don't know."

"And you don't know the name of their silent partner?"

"I'm sorry. Abel would know. But you're not likely to see him again. And I know I sure as hell don't want to see him."

She looked so damn eager to please that I began to feel guilty for making what, after all, was nothing more to her than a show of gratitude into a full-scale exam. So I let up, feeling content with what I'd learned, and changed the subject.

"You're taking off with that big Oakie?"

"Uh-huh." She grinned and her whole body relaxed.

"What does he do for a living—your Bobby?"

"He's got prospects, Harry."

She said it in a way that made me think that she'd said the same thing many times before. For just a second, I think she caught the echo, too. And her dark, handsome face reddened with the memory of all the Abels and the Bobbies and their prospects that never turned out. When she realized that I was thinking the same thing, she blushed more deeply and looked up at me with a touch of defiance in her eyes.

"I better be going," I said quickly. "You take care of yourself, Coral. And if you ever need a detective, give me a call."

"I'll remember that," she said, brightening. "But

we'll be halfway to Colorado by tonight, so it isn't likely we'll be seeing each other again."

I guess, finally, we were both glad of that. We said goodbye. Bobby came stomping onto the porch and pounded on a newel post like a jealous stag sharpening his antlers on a tree trunk. I went out. He went in, slamming the screen door behind him. And I walked back up the marl slope to the car, thinking I'd learned a lot more than I'd expected for one short morning.

# 17

**I DROVE DOWN** to the Riorley Building after finishing with Coral. There was exactly one letter beneath the mail slot on the anteroom floor—a bulk-mailed circular urging me to vote for the right-to-work law— and there was one call on the answer-phone from a woman identifying herself as Ulgine Ruhl. Ulgine spoke with the sweet, nasal lilt of a soloist in a Baptist church choir. "I wanchu to find my Wilmer for me," she began. "'Cause . . ." And that was it. She must have changed her mind about Wilmer in the middle of the sentence, when she couldn't think of one good reason why she wanted him back. I was proud of her. Wilmer was no good—a high-stepper with a checked tam and a gold eye-tooth and a taste for the booze and the ladies. She was better off without him.

I spent a quarter of an hour running through

scenarios for the evening—how I would time my disclosures and how much I would disclose. I was feeling so good I decided that I wouldn't even bother bringing a photograph. I would simply go with what I already knew and make them guess about the hard evidence.

Around two I walked down to the coffee shop in the lobby and traded stories with Lou Billings, my dentist, who has an office on the third floor of the Riorley. Preston LaForge seemed to be the topic of every conversation in the room, which wasn't surprising; and eventually Lou got around to him, too. Jim Dugan, a courthouse lawyer who also has an office in the Riorley, dropped by just as Lou began to theorize about LaForge's motives.

"I'll tell you, Lou," he said. "Something's not kosher about the whole thing."

"Why do you say that?" I asked him.

"Scuttlebut." Dugan leaned across the table and whispered, "They found some strange gear in La-Forge's apartment. But the Bengals' brass is trying to keep a lid on it. Looks like he was a little . . ." Dugan rotated his hand in that classic gesture of equivocation.

Lou sat back in his chair and looked hurt. "No. I don't believe it. Not LaForge."

Dugan shrugged. "I'm just telling you what I heard. And I'll tell you something else. He wasn't alone last night when he did it. He had company."

I squirmed a little in my chair. "Are they saying who?"

Dugan shook his head and jabbed at his horn-rim glasses with a meaty forefinger. "Could be they're not saying for the same reason they're not talking about what they found in his bedroom."

That was enough to get me interested.

I told Lou I had an appointment to keep, paid my chit, and walked uptown to the Courthouse.

It was a lazy Monday on Courthouse Square. Outside of a guard or two manning the gazebo-like information booth on the first floor, there was very little traffic inside the arcade. There wasn't much doing on the second floor either. Most of the old hands from the D.A.'s office were out for lunch, but I did spot one familiar face, Carrie Harris's, coming out of an office marked "Private."

"Long time no see," I called to her.

She stopped in front of the frosted glass door and glared at me with foot-tapping impatience.

We'd never been good friends, Carrie and I. We'd never hit it off. She was bright, bitchy, and pretty in a smug, aggressive way—one of those attractive women whose charm and beauty, are as depthless as stamped tin, the kind whose dark speculative eyes are always finishing conversations before they've begun. In the six years since I'd quit working in the same office with her, she'd found a suitable object for her attention—a young assistant D.A. named Harris, who had a thin crocodilean smile and a solid political future. But old grudges die hard. And I could see from the bare tolerance on Carrie's face that she hadn't forgotten the bad feeling between us.

"Got a minute?" I asked her.

She glanced at her watch. "Maybe half of one."

"I hear you got married. Congratulations."

She shrugged, just as I thought she would. The ring was already chafing her finger, and that gave me something to work with.

"Marriage not all it's cracked up to be, huh?" I said sympathetically.

She smiled a tight-lipped smile and ducked her head. She couldn't pass up the opportunity to complain, not Carrie.

I took her by the arm and she looked suitably mortified; then she struggled with her conscience for half a second and won; and down we went, the spider and the fly, to the Courthouse coffee shop to talk over old times and new.

By the time Carrie and I had finished our talk it was close to four. I'd heard all about Dick, about what a well-hung beast he was and about how Carrie kept feeling that there had to be something "more" —meaningful glance— to a man-woman "thing." Not that she was a prude. Far from it. She loved sex and she loved to do it in funny places and she was always protected. And, so on.

I got a little hot under the collar. I'll admit it. Carrie Harris was a sexy lady and she liked to flaunt it. She was also personal secretary to Walker Parsons, the district attorney. Between intimacies, I managed to pump her about Preston LaForge.

They knew all about Preston down at the D.A.'s office. He had quite an arrest record. Indecent carriage. Soliciting minors. D & D's. Window peeping. Just about every unsavory misdemeanor on the books. But there had been no convictions, because none of the charges brought against Preston had ever been pressed. He'd been too valuable to the Bengals and to the city; so he'd gotten away with a handslap and a promise to behave.

I could have guessed that much from what I'd seen of him. What I would have had trouble guessing was what the cops had found in his bedroom. Good old Preston had kept a photo collection of his own on the dresser. And chief among his mementos were snapshots of an unknown sixteen-year-old girl with a thin, avaricious face. There were dozens of them, Carrie said. Most picturing carnal and sadistic acts between the girl and Preston.

What I never could have guessed was what they found with those photographs.

On the dresser, beside the cache of photos, was a little note in Preston's childlike hand. The gist of it was that he had murdered the girl in the pictures one drunken night, mutilated the body, dropped it in the murky Ohio, and now felt so guilty about what he had done that he couldn't live with himself. And, so, he had bid the world goodnight, had Preston LaForge.

There was some indication that the apartment had been visited after Preston had gone to his reward. But, aside from that, the Preston LaForge suicide seemed to be a closed case. In fact, the D.A. was getting a court order that very afternoon to start dredging the Ohio down by the locks.

"There's no chance that the suicide was faked, is there?" I said, trying to sound cool and casual and not doing a very good job of it. "That the note was forged?"

She shook her head. "The forensic team went over the whole place three times. They wanted to be sure. Walker told them to make absolutely sure." She wrinkled her nose. "You wouldn't believe how disappointed he was when the ballistics team and the coroner and the handwriting people said that murder was out. Can you imagine how much hay he could have made out of prosecuting Preston La-Forge's murderer? Preston LaForge, for Christ's sake! He walked around all morning in a black funk. It was as if he'd lost the nomination for governor."

"And the other people in the house—the ones who arrived after the suicide?"

"We don't know for sure. But it appears they didn't stay for more than a few minutes. Just time enough to spot the body and vamoose."

"Nothing was taken?"

She shook her head. "Why are you so interested, Harry?"

"Well, after all," I said with grim humor. "Preston LaForge!"

"It is hard to believe, isn't it?" Carrie said. "You'd think a man like that could have found other ways to amuse himself."

"Yeah. You'd think so."

"There's probably no chance of finding the body now. That's what Dick says. Not after a week or so in the river. There are so many backwaters and marshy spots and things. It'll probably pop up by itself a year from now—all slick and bloated." She shivered and pressed my hand for comfort. "I wonder who she was?"

"Just a girl," I said with a heavy heart. "Who was very unlucky."

"I guess so," Carrie Harris said.

———

I got back to the office around four-thirty. Although I'd been expecting it, Cindy Ann's murder had shocked me. Preston LaForge just hadn't seemed as if he'd had that kind of violence in him. Crazy he had been, without a doubt. But crazy enough to murder a teenage girl? To mutilate her body? Then to pretend that he was going to rescue the girl he himself had killed? That was crazy with a big C, as a psychiatrist friend once put it. But, then, I was being crazy with a little c to dispute what was indisputable. The girl was dead. LaForge was dead by his own hand, with a note of apology pinned to his sleeve. Even a die-hard sentimentalist, suspicious of any theory that confutes what the heart and the gut say must be so, balks at the cold fact of death.

I hesitated a minute before picking up the phone. But I couldn't con myself this time with the pleasant fiction that she might still be alive. It would have come to this anyway, I told myself. Whether it had been Preston or the Jellicoes or anyone else. Sooner of later, he'd have had to face the truth. And, sooner or later, you would have had to tell him.

Hugo's son, Ralph, answered the phone.

"Hello!" he said buoyantly. "I guess you want to talk to Dad."

"Look, Ralph," I said. "I've got some very bad news for him."

"Oh," he said and the good spirits vanished. "It's that girl, isn't it? The one he hired you to look for?"

"Yeah," I said. "She's dead, Ralph."

"Oh, my God." There was a moment of silence and then he said, "I guess he'll have to know."

"He's sure to find out. They're keeping a lid on it now, but my guess is that it'll make the papers in a day or so."

"How did she . . . how did it happen?"

"She was murdered. It's very ugly, Ralph."

He sighed heavily. "Should I tell him?"

"No," I said. "I think I should. But not over the phone. I'll come up there tomorrow morning."

"All right," he said. "I'll make sure he's around. There's nothing you want to say to him now, is there?"

"No. It'll be hard enough tomorrow."

I hung up the phone and leaned back in the chair. She hadn't been much, Cindy Ann Evans. Venal, manipulative, sick in mind and soul. But she'd had what Preston had called a "sweetness," which

probably meant a simple and fatal pliability to La-
Forge, but which to me suggested the beginnings of
a heart—that decency that Hugo had loved about
her and that even hard-bitten Laurie Jellicoe had
granted her. Whoever she had been, she hadn't deserved to die in the way she had. And she hadn't
deserved to be served up to that death by a pair of
middle-class pimps and their silent partner, all of
whom were scrambling desperately, now that she
was gone, to disassociate themselves from her murder. That's why they wanted those damn pictures
back so badly. They didn't want any evidence floating around that could connect them with the murdered girl and through her with Preston LaForge.
That's why they'd searched the apartment—to get
rid of anything that might lead the police to them.
Murder investigations have a nasty way of prolifer-
ating. They're dangerous and unpredictable things,
especially dangerous if you happen to be accessories
before the fact.

Well, I was still working for Hugo Cratz. At least,
until the morning. And I thought it would do us
both some good to see the Jellicoes behind bars.
That little man inside me was wide awake and calculating like mad.

The thing to do was to make sure they stayed in
town long enough for the police to build a case
against them. Because it seemed certain that once
they'd tied up the loose ends they would make a
discreet exit. Disconnect the answering machine in
their Plum Street office, blackmail a few selected

customers into forgetting that Escorts Unlimited had ever existed, change their names, dye their hair, go underground for a few years and resurface in another place to run the same seedy scam. And the truth was that they could easily get away with it. As long as no one could connect them to LaForge or Cindy Ann, the Jellicoes and their partner would escape scot-free.

So I had to freeze them by keeping them guessing about the photographs. And, in the meantime, I had to turn up a witness who'd be willing to testify to the kind of organization that the Jellicoes ran. Tracy Leach would be perfect, if he'd cooperate. And maybe he would, once he learned why Preston had killed himself. That is, if he didn't already know why Preston had blown his head off, if he hadn't been a part of the whole ugly business to begin with.

# 18

**I'D HOPED TO** get to the Busy Bee early, just to check things out. Not that I'd expected to be ambushed by the Jellicoes in the restaurant. That would be preposterous madness, especially if I was right and all they were interested in was getting out of town as quickly and cleanly as possible. But there was always a chance that they were as preposterously mad as Preston LaForge had turned out to be. So I took a long, careful look around before getting out of the Pinto.

I'd taken the precaution of bringing a gun along with me—a .45 caliber Colt Commander with a nickle-plated barrel, which is the only weapon I keep in the downtown office. I had it strapped in a shoulder holster under my left arm. And I had a micro-cassette recorder with a built-in condenser mike in my coat pocket. If Laurie proved as talkative as Lance had been on Sunday night, I wanted to get what she had to say down on tape. Of course, what I recorded would never hold up in open court, but it might be enough to interest the D.A. and a grand jury.

When I was sure that no one was lurking around the lot, I got out of the car and walked briskly up the alleyway to Ludlow and turned left onto the sidewalk and left again into the Busy Bee.

Jo was standing by the door as I walked in. She looked pleased and flustered when she turned around, menu in hand, and saw me smiling at her.

"You know I'm not off until ten tonight," she said.

"So? A man has a right to eat, doesn't he?"

She whirled demurely around. "Right this way, sir."

I pinched her on her pretty butt and one of the waitresses barked with laughter. *"Harry,"* she hissed.

Jo put me at a table in the rear of the room, beneath the bar. "I'll get you a drink," she said. She'd started up the three steps to the bar level when I grabbed her hand.

"I'm going to be having some company, Jo," I said. "Laurie Jellicoe."

"In here? Tonight?"

I nodded. "Any second."

"There isn't going to be any trouble, is there, Harry? I mean you're not in any danger, are you?"

"No."

"I don't believe you," she said under her breath.

Jo walked up to the bar and came back down a minute later with a Scotch, which she smacked down in front of me.

"Just watch it," she said.

"I'll do my best, lady."

Someone started calling my name from the front of the restaurant. *"Har-ee! Har-ee!"*

I didn't even have to look up. If I'd heard that voice over the phone, I would have asked to speak to her daddy. It was that fulsome. By all rights, it should have gone with floppy hats and big white beads and print dresses that spangled like oil spilled on water. But, aside from her show girl's smile, Laurie Jellicoe just didn't fit the part. Not that she wasn't dressed to kill. On that night she'd left Cardin in the closet: tight lamé blouse with a good deal of pretty brown cleavage showing and black silk slacks that barely made it over her rear. She'd dressed with cold professional skill. And the impression I was supposed to take away from it and the smile in her fruity voice was that we were way past the first name basis now. We were pals. Instead of exciting me, Laurie Jellicoe made me nervous and very suspicious.

*"That's* her?" Jo whispered. *"That's* Laurie Jellicoe?"

"This is beginning to sound like *Shane*," I said with a laugh. "Go up to the door, darlin', and usher the poor girl in."

Jo tugged at the bodice of her dress and stalked

off to the front of the restaurant. I reached into my coat pocket and flipped on the recorder.

It didn't look as if Jo had exchanged any words with the Jellicoe girl as she guided her to my table. But Laurie's smile had become a pinched, joyless grimace by the time she sat down. Jo flapped a menu in front of her, and Laurie kept smiling with effort, as if that toothy grin were painted on her face for all time. As soon as Jo walked off, Laurie turned to me, still smiling, and said, "I'd like to get that cunt alone for ten minutes," in the sweetest little girl voice imaginable.

"What did she say to you?" I said with real curiosity.

Laurie only laughed—the belle-of-the-ball laugh. "It doesn't matter."

She reached inside her purse for a pack of cigarettes, but her hand was shaking violently. I held her hand to steady it. She giggled mindlessly and ran a long-nailed finger down my palm.

"You know, I like you," she said. She shook her hair a bit for effect and breathed out a cloud of white smoke. Behind that cloud her eyes were bright and devilish. "It's a shame I didn't meet you before I tied up with Lance. We could have made nice music together. I like to blow things."

"I'll bet you do."

"U'm." She puckered her lips with lazy sensuality and blew a smoke ring across the table. "Maybe we should get out of here," she said, glancing jealously at the bar where Jo was perched like a bird of prey.

"We have to talk first."

"We've got time for that. Let's go up to the park and talk. It'll be dark in an hour. We can talk then. C'mon. I swear it's not a set-up, if that's what you think. Let's take in a little nature."

"I don't think your boy, Lance, would like that."

She snorted. "God, Lance and I aren't even talking anymore. Much less . . ."

"Why?" I said.

"Why what?"

"Why aren't you two talking anymore?"

"Preston," she said wearily. "He's angry about Preston."

"What about him?"

She put a finger to her lips. "I'm not a fool, Harry, honey. I didn't come here to tell secrets."

"What did you come here for?"

"The pictures. That's what Lance thinks, anyway. But we can talk about them later. I need a lover right now."

"Why me?"

Laurie looked sulkily into my face. "Because!" she said with mock-petulance. "I need you. Isn't that enough?"

I shook my head, and she gave me just the shadow of a grin. "You're an odd man, Harry Stoner. A couple of days ago you were undressing me with your eyes."

"I've grown up a lot in the last few days."

"All right," she said. "Say I'm lonesome, then. Say this has been a very lonely and very bad week for everybody. And I need someone to pretend I'm in love with. Is that O.K.?"

"What do I get out of it?"

She looked at me with astonishment. "You put a mighty high value on yourself, mister. What do you *want* out of it?"

"Cash," I said. "Say twenty thousand dollars."

"Listen, Dillinger," she said. "I don't have to pay anybody to make love to this." She looked down at her body as if it were something detached and arrayed on a pedestal. "You can go to hell with your lousy cracks."

"The money's not for you, Laurie. I wouldn't know how to set a price on that."

She glared at me savagely. "For what, then?"

"For the pictures. You know, the ones with you and Lance and poor Cindy Ann in them?"

"What do you mean *poor* Cindy Ann?"

"Didn't you know, Laurie? She's dead. Preston killed her."

Some of the anger left Laurie Jellicoe's face. "You know about that?"

"Yep. I got friends at the D.A.'s office."

"I see," she said. "Twenty thousand dollars is a lot of money."

"Yes, it is. But if you don't come up with it, I'll have to go to the police."

"We wouldn't like that."

"I wouldn't like to do it myself." I patted her

hand. "I'd hate to see something as good as you end up in the can."

She giggled nervously. "Would be kind of a waste, wouldn't it?"

"So, I want the money, Laurie. And, because I know how people can be, how antsy they can get at times, I want some security, too. You see I have the feeling that if I was to turn those pictures over to you, me and my twenty thousand dollars wouldn't be around very long."

"What would it take to make you feel secure?"

"A few names. A few details about how you run your business. The name of your partner . . . yeah, I know about him, too, Laurie. What I want is a deposition that I can file with my lawyer. I mean, just in case. And I want to know exactly where Cindy Ann Evans was dumped."

"We didn't have anything to do with that," she said stiffly. "Preston just went a little crazy. He was always a little crazy, if you ask me."

"She was still one of your girls, Laurie. And I mean *your* girls, baby. The kind you liked to undress and, what shall we say, *play* with."

She didn't blush, not this one. "How do we know you have the pictures?"

"I've got them and a lot more to go with them. You'll just have to take my word for that."

"I don't know," she said. "I don't know if that's good enough."

"It's going to have to be, honey. Either I get that money in the next twenty-four hours along with the information I want, or I'm going to the cops with what I know. And the way they're worked up about Preston LaForge, it won't take them a minute to bust your sweet ass. And, I'd hate to see that, Laurie." I stroked her cheek. "Because it's such a sweet ass."

"It isn't up to us," she said. "I mean, not entirely."

"You mean you'll have to consult your partner. That's all right. Newport's only an hour away."

She flinched and pushed back from the table. "I'll have to talk this over with Lance."

She looked me up and down and sighed. "How 'bout buying me a drink? I need something to do with my mouth, as long as we're not taking that little ride up to Mt. Storm together."

I grinned at her. "O.K. One for the road."

# 19

**WE HAD OUR** drink, Laurie and I. And another. And another. And around a quarter of eight she glanced at her gold Cartier watch and said, "I better be getting back."

She gave me one sweet, lingering smile and murmured, "Too bad."

"Like you once said, another lifetime, maybe."

"I guess so." She stirred the drink with her fingertips. "You know it's funny how people's lives turn out. A few home-town pageants. A couple of rugged years trying to crack the big-time. Some photo spreads and . . ." Her voice trailed off and she frowned.

It was one of those revealing moments when you can see the sixty-five-year-old woman in the twenty-five-year-old girl—the mouth drawn down and wrinkled at the tips, and the skin stretched grimly across the model's high cheekbones, and the bones themselves poking through like things imprisoned in the flesh. I understood suddenly why she smiled all the time, even when the rest of her face was joyless. It was to keep her from looking as old as she felt. I probably would have felt sorry for her, if she'd had better reasons to frown.

She got up from the chair. "See ya," she said. Her mouth opened up and the smile popped back on like a refrigerator bulb. "In that other life."

She walked out of the Bee and I settled back in the booth seat, switched off the tape recorder, which had run out long before, and toyed with the rest of my Scotch. Down the track, I could see some powerful trouble coming. I didn't know who, yet. But it was coming. And that third partner—the one with the final word—was the engineer.

Because it was starting to fall apart between the Jellicoes. Two people were dead. What had begun as a profitable scheme was turning into a nightmare. Given enough time and a little pressure from me, the two of them would be at each other's throats. And whoever that third partner was, if he had any brains at all, he wasn't going to sit around and get eaten alive. No, he'd come after me. And, maybe, after the Jellicoes, too. Of course, the bright side was that, if I survived it, I'd have the whole vile crew where I wanted them—filled with murderous hate and ready to sell each other out for the price of immunity. If I survived.

Jo sauntered up to the table and gave me a peaked grin. "I see little Miss Muffett is gone."

"Just now."

"Leaving the reek of sulphur behind her." Jo sat down across from me. "About what I said this morning . . ." She prodded my fist with a finger. "I take it back."

"You *don't* love me?"

"Not that part. The other. I guess people do what they have to do, and there's no explaining it. I started to think about why I work here at the Bee, about the hundreds of reasons that led me to this place. And the best one I could come up with was that I do what I do because it answers some sense of obligation inside me. I guess your job means the same thing to you?"

"I've always been good at finding things for other people," I said, poking her finger with one of my own. "That's the best I've been able to come up with."

We stared wryly at each other.

"Did she make a pass at you?" Jo said.

"Pass is probably the wrong word. She showed a certain interest."

"The bitch."

"She had some kind words for you, too. What did you say to her?"

"Something about the way she was dressed," Jo said tartly. "I would have liked to have torn her eyes out. She's the one who's responsible for what happened to that little girl, you know."

I hadn't forgotten. I hadn't forgotten that, for a second.

Two very respectable Cincinnatians walked through the door of the Bee and Jo got to her feet. "See you later?" she said hopefully.

"I'll be here," I told her.

The Bee shut down at half past nine. I sat alone in the dining room while the waitresses cleared the tables and smoked and joked and toasted each other with empty Coke glasses. A restaurant is a far cheerier place after the customers have gone. Everyone is loose and clubby. Leftovers are eaten. Drinks are poured. No one wants to go home. It's like leaving a warm, friendly kitchen.

Jo and I spent half an hour chatting with Hank and the bar girls. And, at ten, we sneaked out through the kitchen door. The night air was mild and romantic. And I could feel it like a soft, warm hand on my face. I'd been sorely tempted three times that day, so I wasted no time in driving back to the Delores. I looked so intensely preoccupied that, at first, Jo thought something had gone wrong on the case. I played up to her, putting a tight, maniacal grin on my face and staring madly at the roadbed. But, about halfway home, she caught on. And, by the time I pulled into the lot at the rear of the building, we were both a little drunk and breathless.

We walked, arm in arm, around to the front of

the building. And I had just unlocked the framed-glass front door and was pushing it open with my left hand and pulling Jo with my right when I saw him peer around the bannister of the first landing. I didn't see much of his face. Just that nose like a letter opener and a tuft of coal black hair. He was wearing a blue sweater cap and a light blue wind-breaker over a plaid shirt and jeans.

He couldn't have caught me at a better moment —of course, that was the way it had been planned. And, while I remember what happened next in minute detail, like a slow motion sequence in a Peckinpah film, it only took thirty seconds of actual clock time.

As soon as I spotted him, I whirled around to face Jo. She was smiling, expecting a joke, because that was the mood we'd been in. When she saw my face, her own face knitted in confusion and she started to say something. I pushed her, with all my strength, back out of the hall light. She let out a little yell, as she lost her footing, and went crashing backward into a prickly rose bush. I dove to the opposite side of the stoop just as the first shot went off behind me.

The entire front door flew outward off its hinges, spewing glass and splinters for a good thirty feet up the pathway and leaving a ragged hole where the frame had been. I knew at once that I'd been hit in the back by some of the pellets. But I didn't feel any pain. Just a wetness and a warmth, as if someone had thrown hot broth on my coat.

I landed in the brambles on the left side of the front walkway, face down in the dirt. I could hear Jo crying my name. I reached inside my coat and pulled out the pistol. My hand came away red and slippery. But I wasn't thinking of the pain yet. Or the seriousness of the wound. Gun in hand, I rolled left into the light of the hallway and looked up toward the landing. He was slipping two more shells into the breech. I watched him for a split second. His hands seemed to move with incredible dexterity and yet there was nothing rushed about his movements.

I braced my right arm with my left, just as he was snapping the breech closed. He looked up and spotted me there on the sidewalk, but the shotgun was still facing toward the stairwell. I pulled the trigger of the Colt four times. The gun jumped wildly, leaping completely out of my hand on the fourth shot and skittering across the concrete. God knows where the other three shots went, but one of them slammed into Abel Jones's chest and out his neck. I could see the yellow wall behind him turn red, as if some invisible hand had splashed bright red paint on it. He pitched forward; his head nodded down, so that all I could see were the eyes, bulging whitely from the compression of the bullet he'd taken in the throat.

Then the shotgun in his hands went off with a terrific, smoky blast—straight down into the staircase. The explosion was like a small grenade going off. It bit a huge chunk out of the first three stairs, whirling tile and stone and metal about the hallway like shrapnel, and sent Jones flying backward against the blood-stained wall of the landing, as if he had been jerked on a taut rope. He slumped to his ass and lolled forward, his legs stretched out in front of him, the shotgun lying at the foot of the stairs.

And then there was a terrific silence. With him just sitting there in all that plaster dust and blood. And me, stretched out on the pavement with my gun five feet away from me and a sharp pain beginning to form in my left side.

And then there was noise. Lots of it.

People inside the building were yelling. And Jo was crying "Oh, my God, Harry," in a shrill, broken voice. And lights went on all over the building, so that the little courtyard was lit up like day. Then I could see some man on the landing, looking in horror at the dead gunman. And a woman shrieked from the stairwell. The man on the landing told her to "Shut up!" and stepping over the dead man's legs, worked his way down the broken staircase and out into the yard. He came running over to me and stooped down.

Before he could say anything, I said, "The girl. See about the girl."

He looked over to the rosebush and back at me. "She's all right." He looked at my back and said, "You're wounded."

Good thinking, I said to myself.

Then Jo appeared.

Her face was bleeding at the hairline and the

blood had run down one cheek. The rest of it was chalk white and so twisted with emotion that it didn't look like Jo's face.

"Do something!" she shrieked at the man.

"I'm doing my best, lady. There's an ambulance coming." He looked down at me and said, "How does it feel?"

"It hurts," I said.

"Oh, God!" Jo stamped her feet furiously.

"I'm O.K., honey," I said to her. "Really. I'm O.K."

She looked down at me and started to cry.

"I've taken a few pellets in my left side," I said to her. "It's not serious. I've been shot before, so I know. Unless I go into shock, I'll be O.K. The fact that it hurts is good. If it were a more serious wound, I wouldn't feel anything for an hour or so."

"How can you be so calm?" Jo screamed at me.

"What do you want me to do? Get hysterical? I'd get up, but I'm not sure I haven't broken some ribs."

"Just stay there," the man said, urging me back with his hands.

For some reason, Jo thought that that gesture was funny. She laughed and wiped a little blood off her face. Then she kneeled down and kissed me on the lips.

"I love you," she said, wiping the hair from my forehead.

"And I love you."

She glanced back over her shoulder at the stairwell and got a sick look on her face. "Oh, my God," she said quietly.

I touched her hand. "Don't look at him."

"He wanted to kill you."

"He damn near succeeded."

She looked back down at me. "He's dead."

Sirens and flashing blue lights filled the street. Two white-clad ambulance attendants lifted me onto a stretcher and put a blanket over me. With Jo holding my hand, they carried me out to the ambulance.

"Did you see the guy in the hallway?" I heard one say to the other.

"Yeah," he said. "Sweet Jesus, what a mess."

# 20

THREE PELLETS WERE embedded in my back, in an ellipsis that stretched from below my left arm pit to about an inch from the spine. The shot hadn't entered deeply enough to do any more than tear the latissimus dorsi. The biggest problem, the intern explained, as I was being wheeled into surgery at Cincinnati General, was the chance of blood poisoning.

"That and the police," he said gravely. "I understand you killed a man tonight."

"What would you do if someone pointed a sawed-off shotgun at you and pulled the trigger?"

He didn't answer.

It took about ten minutes of probing with forceps to get the pellets out. I didn't feel any pain; they'd given me a shot of Xylocaine. But I could hear the sound the pellets made as he dropped each one into a metal tray and could feel the dull purchase of the suturing needle as it passed through my flesh. When the intern was through, a nurse put me on a bottle of glucose and wrapped some gauze and an Ace bandage around my middle. Then she and the intern wheeled me up to the second floor for observation.

"How long will I be in?" I asked the intern.

"A day or so. There could be some edema or residual shock. We want to keep an eye on you until morning." He took a look at the bandage and said, "You're very lucky. An inch or so to the right and those pellets could have fractured your spine. As it is, you'll have a sore back for a few weeks. And you won't be using your left arm for awhile. At least, not for heavy lifting. But, aside from that, you should be as good as new."

"How is Jo?" I asked him. "The girl who came in with me?"

"She had a nasty cut on her scalp and some bruises and lacerations on her arms and legs. But there's no sign of fracture or concussion. She should be fine."

"Can I talk to her?"

"I'll see." He walked out of the room.

About an hour later, a short ugly man in a brown business suit walked in. "Lieutenant Alvin Foster," he said, drawing a chair up beside the bed. "I'd like to ask you a few questions."

Foster was in his late forties, balding in horns that curved around a thatch of thin black hair. He had a jowly, big-pored face, five o'clock shadow, yellow teeth, dark-ringed green eyes, and the kind of thick lips that look like lozenges of hard rubber that someone has knicked with a penknife. He smelled strongly of tobacco and after-shave, and he spoke in a thin, crackling tenor. Like Walter Brennan's scratchy voice, only huskier and not as whiney.

He looked at me unpleasantly, then took a pack of crumpled Tareytons out of his pocket. "I guess they won't mind," he said, shaking a cigarette from the pack. He lit it and puffed a white cloud of smoke toward the floor. "I understand you used to be on the force."

"Just the D.A.'s office," I said.

He waved his hand. "Same difference. This guy you wasted, do you have any idea why he was trying to drop you?" He didn't let me answer. "It was a professional job." He explained it to me with his hands. "He's sitting on the landing. He tells a neighbor that he's waiting for you. The neighbor doesn't know different—why should he? But the guy knows where you live and when you're coming home and how you'll be coming through the door. From the landing, it's a sweet set-up. Four steps up and a bannister to lean it on. And maybe a thirty degree angle down, so he's sure to take your legs off even if he don't get off a timely shot. And what're you going to do when you make him? You got your hands full of door and keys and that girl. It's like shooting fish in a barrel." He clapped his hands together and looked at me with lively malice. "You should be dead."

"I was lucky. I spotted him before he got the gun set, just as he was peeking around the bannister."

"Lucky don't cover it," Foster said. "Were you expecting his kind of company?"

"No."

He dropped the cigarette to the floor and crushed it out with his heel. "We got a problem, then."

"Look, why don't you call up Bernie Olson on the D.A.'s staff. He'll tell you what kind of man I am."

"Uh-huh." Foster reached painfully inside his coat, as if he were about to scratch himself. Instead, he pulled out a small photograph of Cindy Ann Evans. One of *my* photographs. "We found this on the guy. He had about twenty of them in his pocket. Does that mean anything to you?"

I thought it over quickly. Jones had robbed the apartment before ambushing me. The police wouldn't have any trouble putting that much together. The rest of it—the why of it—was what he was waiting to hear. It was just a question of how much I wanted to let him know.

"Her name is Cindy Ann Evans. I was hired to locate her."

"Having any luck?" he said coyly.

"Not yet. She's disappeared."

"Who hired you?"

"That's privileged information."

"Bend the rules a little," he said with an ugly edge in his voice.

"Sorry."

"All right, we'll skip that for the time being. The guy who shot you, do you know who he was?"

"Never saw him before in my life."

"His name is Jones. Abel Jones. He's a low-life from Riverview. He loan sharks on the West Side. And he wasn't the type to kill unless there was a dollar in it. So it looks like we got someone with a powerful grudge against you. So powerful he's willing to shell out five grand for a contract. Any ideas who that could be?"

"In my line of work," I said casually, "you make enemies."

Foster eyed me coldly. He knew I wasn't telling him the truth, and he wanted to punch me for it. In another place, at another time, he probably would have punched me. Cops hate a lie worse than sin and love to catch folks telling them. Like evangelists, they make a living off depravity and they need to have their prejudices confirmed from time to time. It gives them a lift.

"O.K., Stoner," he said. "We'll talk again."

"Any time, lieutenant."

He passed a hand through that thatch of black hair. "I don't know who you think you're protecting, but we have reason to believe that the girl in that picture was murdered."

I tried to look surprised.

"No," he said lightly. "That won't cut it." He started for the door. "You think about it for a few days. See if you can't remember why someone tried to kill you. Because they're going to try again. And, next time, fella', you won't be so . . . lucky."

He was absolutely right. And the sane part of me was pleading, "Tell him the whole thing." But that was the sane part. The other seventy-five percent kept feeling Laurie Jellicoe's hand stroking mine and hearing her sweet urgent voice swearing that it wasn't a set-up and seeing that shotgun go off like a wind-blown torch and all that glass and debris flying out at me like a crystal wind and smelling the cordite smoke afterward and the sweet tang of blood. I just didn't get shot all that often. I didn't have to toss my lover bodily into a thornbush and pray that she wasn't lying dead in the dirt of a bullet wound.

And then there was the thought of Preston, bleeding on that cream-colored rug. And of Cindy Ann, puffing up in the river water like dough rising in an oven. And the plain old reflex stubbornness that comes over me when a cop tries to push me around. Coupled with the intuition, born of years of experience, that, if I turned it over to Foster without giftwrapping it with a bow, he would certainly blow the case. And, with it, any chance I might have of visiting justice on the Jellicoes, if justice was the right word.

I dozed in the hospital bed, high on Xylocaine and fantasies of revenge, and dreamed gruesomely about what I would do when I caught up with Lance and Laurie and their silent partner.

Some time during the night, Jo came in the room and called my name. But it wasn't until the next morning, when the anaesthetic had worn off and the pain began to bite at my back, that I was healed enough in mind and spirit to answer her.

I opened my eyes and saw her sitting in a plastic lounge chair beside the door. There was some sun in the room, coming through the drapes by the window. I took a deep breath and the keen smell of the disinfectant blown through the air-conditioning ducts made me momentarily giddy.

I tried lifting my left arm. It went up, but it hurt mightily. I managed to stretch it out far enough to snag the phone on the nightstand by the bed. According to the Provident Bank time lady, it was ten-thirty A.M. on Tuesday the twelfth and the temperature outside was eighty-eight degrees. Jo heard me hang up the phone and sat up in the chair. She had a gauze bandage on her forehead and there were some splotches of iodine on her arms and on her legs below the hemline of that floral print dress. But she still looked brownly pretty, in a wounded and bedraggled way. Like Ava Gardner playing the nurse in *Snows of Kilimanjaro*. Heart-shaped face, coal black hair, olive skin, gray eyes—all sleepy and concerned.

She smiled at me—a pained, visitor's smile. And I felt compelled to tell her that I wasn't about to die.

"I know that." She ran her eyes up and down my body and they filled with tears.

She got up, and walked over to the bed, and I pulled her down beside me and kissed her.

She looked away for a second. And I could see her seeing Abel Jones, lying in the wreckage of the lobby.

"It couldn't be helped," I said.

She nodded quickly. "I know. But that doesn't make it any less awful." She took a deep breath and looked back down at me. "A man named Foster asked me some questions about those pictures you showed me."

"What did you tell him?"

"I told him to talk to you. I told him I didn't know anything about them."

"You told him right," I said.

"He didn't believe me. You are going to tell him about the Jellicoes, aren't you?"

"When I'm ready."

"That's crazy." She smiled uncertainly. "You want them to try to kill you again?"

"I'd like to see them try," I said grimly.

"You *are* crazy!" Jo's gray eyes flashed and she hopped off the bed. "I'm going to the coffee shop," she said with disgust. "I can't take any more of this macho crap on an empty stomach."

"Just don't wander too far off," I said. "I intend to get out of here by noon."

She looked like she was about to tear her hair. "You're *shot*," she said between her teeth, like she was explaining something for the umpteenth time to a very stupid child. "You're wounded. You can't get up, champ. You're down for the count."

"I'm getting up," I said between *my* teeth.

"Madness!" She turned on her heels and marched out of the room.

At eleven-fifteen, the young intern who had treated me the night before came by. "How's the patient?" he said in a chipper voice. He looked at a clipboard. "Looks like you're going to live. Does it hurt much?"

"Enough," I said.

"It will for awhile. We'll give you some codeine to help kill the pain. If it cramps on you, you may also need a muscle relaxant."

"Would it kill me to leave here this afternoon?"

"It wouldn't kill you, no. I think you'd be better off waiting till tomorrow morning. To be on the safe side."

"I want to live dangerously."

He shrugged. "Let's take a look."

He examined the wound, put some fresh gauze on my back and rewrapped the Ace bandage. "I guess it'll be all right if you want to leave."

He had the nurse get me a prescription and a fresh supply of bandages and he warned me that I would get some drainage and that I shouldn't be alarmed and he cautioned me against overexerting myself. And we shook hands. And that was that.

At high noon, I took an elevator down through the sanitized hospital air, stepped out into the lobby, walked over to the coffee shop window and rapped on the glass.

When she saw me, she looked down at her cup of coffee and shook her head.

# 21

**AT TEN AFTER** twelve, Jo and I caught a Yellow Cab in front of the hospital on Goodman Street and had the cabbie drive us down Burnett to the Delores. It was a very short trip—maybe a mile and a quarter—and the driver, a black man with a grizzled beard and a little brown bald spot on the back of his head, wasn't too happy about the fare.

"Hell, you could've walked this easily," he said, as he pulled up in front of the apartment building. "Big strong man like you."

"I'm an eccentric millionaire," I said, handing him a couple of dollars.

For a few seconds, Jo and I just stood there on the sidewalk and stared at each other—me with my box of gauze and my bag of prescriptions in my right hand and my left arm dangling uselessly at my side, and Jo in her rumpled, dirt-stained print dress

with that bandage on her forehead and all those iodine stains on her arms and legs. I started to laugh,
but she eyed me grumpily.

"It's not funny. You could be dead. I could be
dead. It's not funny."

"I guess not," I said. "Although it sure feels good
to be alive this beautiful morning."

She mumbled something about cats and their
lives, and we walked up the walkway into the
shadow of the building, where broken glass still peb-
bled the ground like rocksalt. Someone had cleared
away most of the large-scale debris and piled it in
a dusty, cement-colored stack to the right of the
stoop. The landing had been swept clean, too; the
yellow wall had been washed; and the staircase
patched with boards. There was still a jagged hole
where the door should have been, but, as I walked
through it, I could hear the sounds of someone
hammering and planing in the basement. I stuck
my head around the door beneath the stairwell and
hollered down, "Leo?"

The sounds stopped immediately, and a hammer clattered to the floor, and someone cursed viciously. Old Leo, the handyman, rumbled up the
stairs, in his denim overalls and white T-shirt, his
belly swinging like a sack of meal above the belt he'd
tied around his hips.

"Oh, it's you," he said in a brittle voice. "It ain't
enough you got to blow up the first floor, you don't
need to take ten years off my life by yelling. You
'bout scared me to death, just now." He took a

polka-dot bandana out of his back pocket and mopped his sweaty face. "I swear, two-thirds of my life just passed before my eyes."

"Which two?" Jo said over my shoulder.

"The first and the last," he said with a wink. "There's a long time in between there I don't like to think about."

He snorted with laughter and started back down the stairs.

"Hold up!" I said to him. "I wanted to ask you something."

"Yeah?" He cocked his arm on the door frame and looked at me impatiently. "I got work to do, you know."

"Last night, after I'd gone off to the hospital, did I have any more visitors? Maybe a tall guy with cowboy boots? Or a pretty blonde who looks like Farrah Fawcett?"

"Oh I'd have remembered that," he said with a roll of his belly. He glanced at Jo and blushed to the roots of his tow-haired scalp. "The answer's no. No one last night a'tall. Though there was somebody asking after you this morning. A sweet young thing with blonde hair. He smelled like a lilac bush."

"Leach," I said to myself.

"He said he had to get in touch with you. I think he left a note in your box. Now, if you don't mind, I got work to do—cleaning up after your damn mess."

As Leo ambled off down the stairs, Jo put a hand

to her mouth and whispered, "Is he always like that?"

"Always."

I opened the mailbox and took out Tray's note. Leo was right—it did smell like lilac water.

Jo peeked at the note. "'*Got* to see you, Tray.'"

"He's *my* friend," I lisped.

She laughed and jabbed me in the side.

The wrong side. I groaned and dropped the bag and box.

"Oh, God, I'm sorry," she said and started to laugh.

I glared at her. "*That* you think is funny?"

She put on a straight face, but her lower lip kept trembling with laughter.

I scooped the stuff off the floor with another groan. "Being alive she thinks is serious business. A man in pain she laughs at."

We got up to the third floor and, when I unlocked the front door, Jo gasped, "My God!" I dumped all the junk on the couch and went into the kitchenette and fixed myself a Scotch.

"Me, too," Jo called out.

I poured another and walked back in and surveyed the damage.

"Abel Jones did not have a delicate touch."

The room was a shambles. Drawers open, their contents scattered everywhere. Bookshelves ransacked. Cushions torn off chairs. I flipped on the Globemaster and sat down on the couch and stared glumly at the wreckage.

"It's just as bad in there," Jo said from the hall. She unzipped her dress and let it fall forward down her arms. "I guess I better start cleaning up."

I took a look at her, standing there half-dressed and eyeing the room with housewifely calculation. Her bra was low-cut and wispy, and the tops of her breasts and the pink rounds of her nipples showed through it.

I leaned back on the couch and took a long pull of the Scotch. "What condition is the bed in?" I said.

She laughed. "What condition are you in?" she said dryly.

She stepped out of the frock and kicked it into the bedroom and walked in after it, her firm pink ass half-naked above the bikini panties.

I started after her and, by the time I got to the bedroom, she was naked on the bed, her hands tented at her lips and a look of spry expectation on her face.

I took a long look at her and she blushed.

"God, I need you," I said heavily.

She arched her back and hips as I kneeled on the mattress. "Make love to me, Harry," she said as I moved on top of her. "I want you to make me—"

I touched her lips with my fingers, then covered them with my mouth.

———

Forget.
I think that was the word she was about to say.

To wipe it all away in a flash of pleasure, an explosion of glands and muscle and nerve endings.

We'd gone at it, too, in one great roiling, passionate coupling. Pure heat—like a junk rush. Her sex wet with my saliva and her own sticky wetness. And me plunging into her rhythmically. And the only sound the slap of flesh and the small, urgent cries we gave to each other.

And it worked for Jo.

As she climaxed, she put a twisted hand beside her mouth, agape with pleasure, and her head rolled away from mine to the mattress. Then she opened her eyes and they were clear of bitterness and bad memory. "Don't go," she whispered to me.

I lay on top of her, feeling her heart beat slowly and the brine of sweat along my belly and in the hollow of her loins. In a minute or two, I rolled away. Jo curled affectionately beside me and was soon asleep. I stroked her black hair, warm yet and damp from love-making, and pretended that I, too, was emptied of all terror and rage.

But, for me, it wouldn't work. Even as I lay there beside her, I knew that in a minute the pleasure would vanish and, instead of staring off blankly into space, I would be seeing Hugo's juicy eyes or Laurie's erotic ones or be imagining the dead doll's stare of Cindy Ann's eye.

I got to my feet and walked quietly into the living room.

My back hurt—a dull ache, like an earache but

shot with occasional twinges of hot pain. It made me feel sick and old and desperate.

The thing was, I didn't know where to begin. I wasn't even sure if I wanted to begin again—to hold my breath and go under, into that green world of cool, predatory sex and sudden violence.

For a second I toyed with the idea of calling Foster. Only I knew what would happen if I turned it over to him. He'd call Tray Leach, who, faced with public exposure and a court trial, would suddenly forget that he'd ever heard of the Jellicoes or of Escorts Unlimited. As for Lance and Laurie, she would bat her sensuous eyes and he would paw at the turf and grumble about persecution. And their lawyer would produce a writ of *habeas* and, with it, a tax record indicating that Escorts Unlimited was nothing more than a legitimate escort service run by two young people who were being victimized by a brutish detective—who killed a man, by the way, on Monday last—and by a dirty, depraved old man with a screw loose in his noggin. Foster would puff a little cigarette smoke and know that the Jellicoes were lying and that there was nothing he could do about it. Not with Preston LaForge dead and Cindy Ann Evans murdered and not a shred of hard evidence to connect them to the Jellicoes. The D.A. could never get an indictment out of a grand jury on the basis of my testimony alone. Because, as the Jellicoes' lawyer would be sure to point out, my character was easily impeached. After all, I'd tried to blackmail those two young people. Hell, it was down on tape, and the police had the tape recorder, along with my gun and my license.

So, where do you go from here, Harry? I asked myself.

Do you call Tracy Leach and get it all started again? Do you take the chance of getting him and you and Jo killed? Because Foster had been right about that. If they were willing to try once on the basis of a few photographs, they'd be more than willing to try again if I kept pushing.

Or do you let it all slide now? Because now's the time to decide, while you still have that anger going for you. Next week, maybe even tomorrow, it'll be too late.

Damn it! I said and slapped myself stingingly on the thigh. I wanted to know who that third man was. Just for my own peace of mind. So I could tell myself that I'd seen it all, before I stepped away. Or didn't step away.

Hell, who knows what he'll do until he does it?

I picked up the phone and made two calls.

The first was to Ralph Cratz—to tell him that I wasn't going to be able to make it up to Dayton that day.

"It's fine with me," he said. "But I don't think Dad's going to like it. I told him you were going to come up, and he's been trying to get you all morning. He's got it in his head that something's gone wrong—you know how he is. And I'm afraid he might try to go back to Cincinnati."

"Keep him there!" I almost shouted. "For God's

sake, keep him in Dayton! If you don't want to see him hurt or killed, you'll do what I say."

Ralph promised to try. "But you know Dad," he said miserably.

The second call was to Tracy Leach—to find out what he'd been in such a rush to talk about.

"Preston," he said. From the sound of his voice, Tracy Leach was either very angry or very frightened. I couldn't tell which.

"What about Preston?"

"Are you going to make me say it over the phone?" he said with distaste.

I thought about the last time I'd been invited to a private meeting to talk things out and said, "Yes. What about Preston?"

"You're a bastard," Leach hissed. The rest of it was delivered at a clipped, furious pace, like morse code. "Some policemen came here. They asked me about Preston. They said he'd . . . that the Evans girl was dead because of him."

"I know that," I said.

"They said he'd left a note by some pictures." Leach paused. "I didn't tell them but I'm telling you. Preston didn't have any pictures like that. I practically lived in his apartment, so I know. Those pictures weren't his. I don't know about the note. It was in his hand. They showed it to me. But I'm telling you"—his voice peaked shrilly—"Preston did *not* kill that girl."

I shivered where I stood in the hot July sunlight. "He didn't kill Cindy Ann," I said flatly. Not like a question. Like a statement of fact. Trying it out, seeing how it sounded, how it resonated.

"And I can prove it," Tray Leach said. "Now will you come over here?"

"I'll be right over," I said and slammed down the receiver.

# 22

IT WAS THE same overripe, dowager's room, but with a difference. He'd taken the rug up—the one I'd splashed with rose water—and he'd hung black crepe along the walls and put black antimacassars on all of the furnishings; so that, now, it was a dowager's room in mourning.

"For Preston?" I said, fingering the black cloth on one of the armrests of the settee.

Tracy Leach nodded.

He'd decked himself in black, too. Black shirt. Black trousers. Black shoes and socks. Given that impassive, boy-like face, he looked vaguely like César, Caligari's somnambulist.

He looked ridiculous. And so did the room. The combination was as vapid as a belated condolence card. And it made me squirm to see it.

"I said a little prayer for him today," Tray said.

"I'm Catholic. Lapsed, of course. The Church doesn't approve of my sexual preferences. But I still go to mass on a few feast days and, every so often, for confession." He looked at me with ugly self-assurance. "Am I boring you? Sorry, if I am. But, you see, according to the Church, his soul is in hell. I don't know if I believe that or not. But I do know what people can do to you while you are still alive. Or while your memory is. They're going to crucify Preston in the papers. And I will not let that happen. He was a weak man, but he was not a killer. The very idea is absurd. He'd no more have harmed that girl than he would have harmed me. He liked her. He told me so. She had been sweet to him. Sometimes children can be sweet in a selfless way, before they learn who they're not supposed to like or love."

"What did he talk about on Sunday afternoon, when he came to see you?"

"You, of course. And what you had done to him. He didn't know what to do. You see, with an operation like the Jellicoes', if a customer should become, shall we say, dissatisfied, he can never complain to the authorities for fear that Lance or Laurie will retaliate with pictures, tape recordings, films. They have a little something on file for each of their special clients."

"What did they have on Preston?"

Leach leaned forward on the settee. "I'm not sure. He wasn't sure, either."

"I don't understand."

Tray got up and walked over to the big rosewood chiffonier. He opened the top drawer and withdrew a piece of paper and brought it back to the couch. "A week ago last Sunday, Preston went to a party in Louisville. I was invited but declined. You see, the Jellicoes were doing the catering and I haven't done any business with them for some time. I don't care for either one of them. They're vermin and they were ruining Preston's life."

Leach looked up suddenly. "She could be incredibly vicious. Teasing, tormenting. I think she's capable of anything—that one."

"Of killing?" I said.

"Even that. She loves pain and she loves to inflict it. She's extraordinarily artful at what she does. And she can make it go on for hours, until you're begging her for release. Believe me, I know what I'm talking about. That girl frightens *me*. And I'm not easily frightened."

"And Lance?"

"A clod. A piece of Texas farm land. Big and dumb and brutal. But, perhaps, not as brutal as she is. Not in the mind, where it really counts."

"Capable of killing?"

"I don't know. Probably. If he were cornered and saw no other way out. But, then, most of us are capable of killing, given the right circumstances."

He gave me a quick look, and I realized that he knew about Abel Jones. Then, I realized that a lot of people probably did. It would have made the eleven o'clock news on all four channels.

227

"You were telling me about a party?"

"Yes. In Louisville. It was a fund-raiser of sorts. A lot of powerful men were invited. You probably wouldn't believe some of the names."

He mentioned two—a state senator and a local politician with a national reputation.

"It's an open secret," Leach said with a touch of contempt in his mild voice. "That politicians go for the rough trade. They like to be bullied, those strong men. They like to be dominated by their women. And the more powerful they are, the more they love it. It makes them feel powerless, for once. Gives them a taste of mortality that they don't get in their everyday lives."

He was enjoying it, breaking what, I suppose, he thought were my idols. A wicked smile played upon his cruel mouth. "I could tell you stories that would make your skin crawl, about those big, strong, red-blooded American men."

"Why don't you tell me what happened to Preston?"

"I'm getting to it," he said with a nasty laugh. "I just want you to pay a little for your illusions, first. The fund-raiser was early in the evening. About twelve the real party began. Preston never could hold his liquor. He was a lousy drunk, sick and sick-making and, eventually, passed out by the end of an evening. That Monday was no different. He drank and joked and pretended to be one of the guys."

Tray laughed forlornly. "You know I think that's all he ever really wanted.

"About two, the Jellicoes brought the girls and boys on. Preston told me they had them dressed up and their faces made up. They paraded them on a little band box under a reflecting ball, with the room lights down and blue light reflections playing on their faces. He said it was very beautiful in an eerie way, like it was snowing a melancholy blue snow on those beautiful children. Cindy Ann was among them. Did you ever see her?"

I shook my head.

"I did, once. She was an extraordinary thing. Hair the color of licked red candy and skin the white of lace. Made up with rouge spots and black eye liner and dressed in a gold chemise, she was like some dada-esque creature. An expressionist child. And there was a mischief in her eyes, a wildness. It was really quite stunning. Of course, she was ignorant as mud. And sharp with her tongue. She could curse like a sailor. But she could also be kind and loving in a remarkably adult way. She had a certain tolerance for weakness that was quite endearing. I just saw her that once. At Preston's house. But I think I fell a little bit in love with her, too. Like Preston.

"In any event, she was at the party. And she spent some time with Preston in one of the rooms they'd set up. But Preston got drunk and sick and someone came in and took Cindy Ann out with him. Preston said he couldn't remember who. It was very dark and there were all of those straight-laced types. County and state officials out for a kinky evening.

Then they started with the Polaroids and the eight millimeters, like they always did. And some of the children were posing in the white camera lights. Some of them were being used and being photographed. Then Preston blundered into another private room and there were movie lights inside and lots of people standing around. He could hear someone moaning from the bed. He couldn't see her face, but they were masturbating her with dildoes. He watched for a while and then went out and drank some more and passed out."

"That's it?" I said. "That's all of it?"

"Not quite. Something happened while he was out. Something terrible. Laurie woke him up by throwing water in his face. The room was empty when he woke and he could see some dawn light through the drapes. Laurie poured coffee into him and told him that he had to get out of there—that something awful had happened to one of the girls. When he asked her what, she looked at him strangely, as if he were playing a game with her. You see, they wanted to make him think that he'd been involved, and he was impressionable enough to take the hint.

"He came to me that Tuesday morning, in tears. And I made him sober up and clean up. Then I made him tell me the whole story, just as I'm telling it to you. I kept asking him what had happened to the girl. And he kept saying, 'I can't remember, Tray. I was in that room and then I was passed out and then Laurie came along with the water.' He was

very frightened. He was afraid he might have killed
the girl while he was drunk. Poor Preston. He would
repeat anything that anyone told him, and after a
time, he'd forget who had told him and think he'd
made it up himself. I'm telling you he was incapable
of killing another human being. He just didn't have
it in him."

"What's on the paper?" I asked him.

"A confession. I made him write up the story,
just as he told it to me. I meant it as a joke, to show
him how foolish all his fears were when he discovered the truth. But . . . it didn't work out that
way."

"May I see it?"

He handed the paper to me. I read it through
quickly. The hand was childlike—a neat block-print
—the hand of a penitent little boy. It stated very
simply the same story that Tray had told me. And it
was signed at the bottom, Preston LaForge.

I gave the confession back to him and he put it
back in the chiffonier.

"You know that'll never stand up as evidence," I
told him. "It doesn't prove that Preston *didn't* kill
Cindy Ann."

"And chop her up and drop her in the Ohio,"
Leach said sarcastically. "And then go back to the
party and fall down drunk?"

"He could have been lying, Tray. He could have
been using you to salve his conscience."

Leach stared at me with savage contempt. "I
made him swear to me that he was telling the truth.

I made him swear it on the Bible. And I'm telling you that he didn't lie to me. I'm not an idiot. I knew Preston well enough to figure out when he was playing games and when he wasn't. What I told you is the truth."

I took a deep breath and stared at the black bunting on the walls. "All right, I believe you."

"Good," he said. "Now what are we going to do about it?"

I stood up and started pacing the carpetless floor in front of the settee. "Someone must have convinced Preston that he'd killed Cindy Ann. Probably because she was murdered and I was asking embarrassing questions and they needed a patsy to take the fall for her death."

"That's what I think, too. And I know who set him up and who planted those disgusting pictures."

"Laurie?"

"It's her kind of fun," Tray said.

"All right. So, let's say Laurie dropped by Preston's apartment some time before I was scheduled to arrive. She brings the pictures with her and tells Preston he killed Cindy Ann in a drunken rage. Would that be enough to drive him to suicide? You knew the man. What do you say?"

"I don't think so," Leach said. "He was impressionable, certainly. And he was easily manipulated and impulsive. But, I don't think that mere words would have driven him to shoot himself. She must have shown him something terrible—something that broke his spirit. Because when he left here on

Sunday night, he was ready to cooperate with you. When he left here, he really thought he was going to get Cindy Ann back. He was very happy. Like a boy."

"So Laurie shows up and, instead of Cindy Ann, she's brought something—a picture, a slide, something—that makes Preston think he's killed Cindy Ann."

"She must be dead," Leach said.

"Seems likely, although it could have been faked."

"Look," Leach said suddenly. "Would you please sit down! You're driving me crazy pacing around like that."

"Sorry." I plopped down into a creaky Queen Anne chair and Tray's face collapsed with pain.

"That's a valuable antique!" he groaned.

I put my right hand on the armrest, dangled my left, and tried to think of ways to prove that Cindy Ann had not been killed by Preston LaForge. It would have been nice if I could have asked her what had happened to her on that bleary festive night. But how can you ask a dead girl how she died? You can't, I thought, but it gave me an idea.

"When's the last time you did business with the Jellicoes?" I said to Leach.

"Three weeks before that party. Over a month, now."

"Are you still on their preferred list?"

He shrugged. "As far as I know."

I studied his old man-young man face. It was

grim and abstracted. I knew the look. I'd had it on my own face the night before. He'd lost someone he'd loved, and he was meditating revenge.

"How badly do you want to strike back at the Jellicoes?" I said.

"Badly enough."

"Enough to take a chance?"

"What's on your mind?"

"Give them a call. They're still in business. At least, they were as of last night. Place an order for this evening. Take delivery and . . . well, you do what you have to do."

"That's all?"

"That's enough. Remember they're going to be very cautious now. Especially with you, since you were so close to LaForge."

"And where do you fit in?"

"Not in. Out." I pointed through the black bunting to the street. "Right out there. Someone has to deliver the child and someone has to pick him up. And when that someone picks him up, he'll have to take him back to wherever they keep the rest of the children."

Tray Leach's face brightened. "I see. You'll follow him."

"That's it. If Cindy Ann is dead, there will be other children there who knew her and who were at that party. Maybe they know what became of her. The only problem is getting in and getting to talk to one of them."

"That may not be easy, given the current situation."

"Leave that to me," I said. "If I get there, I'll get in. Your job is to make sure that the Jellicoes make delivery. And remember, Tray. If they do get wise to us, whoever comes tonight will be coming to kill you."

# 23

IT WAS ALMOST five o'clock when I got back to the Delores. Jo was up and sitting, Indian-style, in a patch of sunlight on the living room floor, sorting papers into neat stacks. She had a terry robe cinched around her and, in the sunlight, with her black hair disheveled and the white swell of her breast just visible through the folds of her robe, she looked like a teenage girl dreaming over a pile of letters.

"How old are you?" I said to her from the door.

She looked up and squinted in the sunlight. "That's a helluva question to ask a person. I'm twenty-eight. How old are you?"

"Thirty-six."

"It'll never work," she said and looked back down at the stack of papers.

"Find anything interesting?" I walked into the

kitchenette and took the bottle of Scotch and two tumblers from the top of the refrigerator.

"You mean aside from the brass knuckles, the black jack, the machine gun, and the carton of grenades?"

"*Did* you find my pistols?" I said, walking back into the living room.

She pointed distastefully at the desk top. A snub-nosed .38 and a .357 magnum with a checked walnut stock and vented barrel gleamed dully in the sun.

I poured two drinks, handed her one, and plopped down on the couch.

"Anything new?" I said, sipping the drink.

"Hugo called."

I sighed heavily. "That's not new. When?"

"Around four." She looked up and squinted again. "He's back in town, Harry. He wants you to come see him."

"What!" I almost spilled the drink as I slammed it down on the table in front of me. "That stupid old man," I said as I walked to the phone.

"He didn't sound well to me," Jo said. "I'm worried about him, Harry. He said his head had hurt him all the way back from Dayton."

"That's just an act," I said.

"I don't think so. He had me so worked up that I almost called a cab and went over there myself. But I thought I'd better wait for you."

"If this turns out to be one of his cons . . ."

Jo looked at me disdainfully.

"All right. We'll take a look."

While Jo was dressing in the bedroom, I fished through the junk on the floor and located two holsters—a shoulder model and a quick release belt-holster made for a .38. I clipped the belt holster on and glanced at the pistols. Both were relatively clean and fully loaded. I tucked the snub-nosed Police Special at my waist and put the heavier and more lethal magnum in the shoulder holster. Then I stripped off my coat and gingerly worked the harness up over my weak arm and across my back.

"Let's get going," Jo said as she walked back into the room. When she saw me standing there with the harness half-on, her mouth dropped open and she said, "My God."

"Can't be too careful these days," I said with an attempt at a smile.

She wasn't having any of it.

"You're going to get yourself killed," she said with awful certainty, as if it were something she had known all along but never before admitted to herself. "I love you and you're going to get yourself killed." She dropped both arms to her sides and gaped at me in disbelief. "Why?"

I slipped the jacket back on and emptied a box of shells into my coat pocket. "I don't know why," I said.

"Surely you can do better than that?" she said, coloring. "I don't understand. You could turn it over to the police. Why don't you turn it over to the police?"

"Because they'd botch it."

"While you, Harry Stoner, the man they can't keep down . . ." Her voice died. "I love you. Doesn't that mean anything to you?"

"It means everything to me."

"Then why . . ." She scoured her eyes with her palms. "I won't take it," she said flatly. "I've already lost one man to senseless violence. I won't take two."

"You're not making this any easier for me," I said angrily. "I'm doing it because I have to do it. Because I can't just turn my back and pretend that I don't care why a deranged teenager with a soft heart was murdered. Look—three people are dead. One of them at my hands. And if I hadn't been damn lucky last night, it could have been four or five." Suddenly I was very angry. I gripped her by the wrists and glared into her face. "How do you think I felt last night, tossing you in the goddamn bushes and watching that shotgun shell burst behind me and wondering if you were being torn apart by it? Do you think I'd let *anyone* do that to me? Do you? Do you think I'd let anyone try to kill me or someone I love? Do you?"

"You're hurting me!" she squealed.

I dropped her wrists. "Are you coming?"

She didn't look up at me as she swept out the door.

———

We drove in silence over to North Clifton, Jo sitting sternly by the window. Her face rapt and cheerless. Twice I started to apologize, but held back. She didn't want to be disabused and I didn't want to explain it.

It took me ten minutes to get to Cornell. I turned left and drove up that maple-shaded street, full of picturesque houses and calm, tree-filtered sunlight, and pulled into the driveway by the hedge of rosebushes. The air was thick with late afternoon sun and heavy with that dead, ghost-filled silence that had weighed on me five days before, when I'd first driven up Cornell to donate half an hour's time to a crusty old man who'd lost his little girl and didn't know where to find her.

We walked up to the porch, where the swing and the lawn chairs huddled mournfully in the shade, and down that crabbed hallway to Hugo's flat.

I knocked once at the door and it opened under the weight of my hand. The old man must have had another key on him. Or left one with his friend George.

He was sleeping in the chair with the yellow throw. The T.V. was talking to him idly from the flecked metal stand. His face looked pallid and ill.

"Hugo?" I said.

He opened his watery blue eyes and smiled at me. "Hello, Harry."

"Hugo, why didn't you stay in Dayton like I asked you to?"

"Couldn't stand it no more. Too damn loud and busy." He grimaced suddenly and rubbed his temple. "Man, my head hurts."

"You're not playing around Hugo? You're not pulling a trick, are you?"

He smiled through the pain. "No, Harry. No trick this time. I think this time, the trick's going to be on me. I shouldn't have exerted myself like I done. Went and gave myself another stroke."

Jo walked to the telephone on the octagonal table. "I'm calling an ambulance," she said hoarsely.

"Getting loose of that damn Ralph is what done it to me. You know I had to pay one of his snot-nosed kids three bucks to get himself lost for a couple of hours? Ralph's such a milquetoast he got all excited—just like I figured he would—and went off looking for Kevin. Then it was just a matter of getting my bag packed and hiking down to the terminal." Hugo laughed remorsefully. "But I went and lost that damn bag in the depot and made myself sick on the ride sitting in the sun." He closed his eyes and sat back in the chair. "I told you I wasn't going to survive this thing. And I was right."

"If you'd have stayed there, damn it, you'd be O.K."

He opened his eyes and looked over at me. "Did you find her, Harry? Did you find my little girl? Don't lie to me, now, son. It don't make no difference any more. I ain't going to survive this in one piece no matter how you slice it. And I got to know. I got to know while it still makes sense to me. In a few hours, I'm going to be a stalk of celery. I know. It happened like this before. And then the truth won't move me one way or another."

Jo touched his hand and he smiled at her. "Don't get yourself worked up, honey. It may sound strange, but I ain't scared of this anymore. It just don't matter to me. I been to Dayton. I seen what being old is like. Didn't fancy it a bit. Knew I wouldn't. Always been a loner, 'cept for George and Cindy Ann." He swallowed hard. "She's dead, ain't she, Harry? My Cindy Ann?"

I smiled at him and said, "Hell no! She's not dead. If you'd have just stayed in Dayton awhile longer, I would have come up there and told you all about it."

He perked up a bit. "She ain't dead?"

I shook my head. "But you were right about the Jellicoes. They were using her as a prostitute in Newport. It's a long story, but I found out through one of the Jellicoes' other girls that Cindy wanted to quit and run. This friend worked with her in Newport. And helped her get away."

"Where'd she go?"

"The girl says Denver."

A twinge of pain made him grimace. "Boy, I hope you're telling me the truth. Sure enough, she ain't dead?"

"Yep."

"I don't see why she had to run away like that. I'd have protected her from them damn bastards myself."

"I guess she didn't want to see you get hurt," I said softly.

"Could be," he said, thinking it through. "She

was always one to think of others before she thought of herself. You going to be able to find her?"

"I'll find her all right," I said cheerfully.

He chuckled and said, "I believe you will. You'll tell her when you find her that I loved her, won't you, Harry?"

I didn't say anything.

"Here's the ambulance," Jo called from the window.

A minute later, two uniformed attendants knocked on the door. They wheeled a gurney into the room and Hugo said, "Aw hell, I don't need that." He started to get up and sat back, stunned, in the chair. "Well, maybe, I'd better," he said sheepishly.

I helped him out of the chair and over to the stretcher. He was a bag of sticks beneath that cardigan and those loose khaki slacks.

They strapped him on and, suddenly, Hugo looked terribly frightened. "You weren't lying to me, were you, Harry?"

"No, Hugo."

He sighed. "Goddamn, ridiculous way to die, ain't it? Being carried out to it like a cord of kindling. So long, Harry," he said, holding up a hand.

I held it for a few seconds and he smiled that sickly, broken-toothed smile. "Let go of my hand, now," he said softly. "Never was crazy about being touched by another man."

"I'll come visit you tomorrow, Hugo."

"Sure you will," he said.

The attendants took him out the door.

Jo started after them. "I'm going to ride down there with him."

She paused at the door. "I don't suppose it'll do any good to say be careful. Or to try to convince you not to do . . . whatever it is you're going to do?"

I shook my head.

She started to cry. "Then I don't know what to say."

They were wheeling Hugo into the ambulance. Jo squeezed my hand once and whispered, "Goodbye, Harry." Then walked quickly out the door. I watched her from the bay as she climbed in beside Hugo and, in a minute, both of them were gone.

———

I circled among the narrow, San Franciscan streets of Mt. Adams until night fell, then dropped down St. Martin's to Paradrome and up to Ida, where I parked beneath an arching willow some three houses down from Tray Leach's home. I'd bought five styrofoam cups full of coffee at a little grocery on St. Regis, and, as I sat there watching the western sky go purple and then deep blue, I flipped the plastic lid off one of them. It was bad, bitter coffee. But I was feeling numb and disoriented after Cornell Street and I had to keep alert all night long, if I was going to bring this thing off. I had a few bennies in a prescription bottle in my slacks. If worse came to worse, I'd pop them, although I didn't want to have to do that. On speed you think too much of the first thing that comes into your head. I pried the lid off another cup of coffee and sat back in the car seat and tried, unsuccessfully, not to think about Jo or about Hugo Cratz.

Around ten, a yellow Dodge van pulled up in front of Leach's house. It was dark beneath the willows, too dark, at first, to make out the man behind the wheel. I slipped the .38 out of the holster and pulled the hammer back. If anyone got out of that van without a kid on his arm, I was prepared to go charging across the street. I could see the blinds rustle in one of Tray's front windows and then one red door opened and a porch light clicked on. Leach came out on the stoop in a Japanese kimono and sandals and waved to whoever was driving the truck. The driver's door opened and rangy Lance Jellicoe stepped out into the street. He looked around nervously, then held his hand back up to the truck door. A much smaller hand grasped his, and Lance pulled a beautiful little boy into his arms. He smiled broadly at the kid and patted him on the rump. The kid grinned back and Lance lowered him to the ground. The little boy was about twelve, dressed in a T-shirt and short pants. His blonde hair was cut straight across the forehead, like the little Dutch boy's, and he had a vain, pretty, slightly prepossessed face—Tray's face, but thirty years younger. The boy ran around the rear of the van and up to Tray's door. Tray said something to him and he laughed. Leach took his hand, waved with the other to Jellicoe, and guided the boy into his house. The porch light went off, the red door closed, Jellicoe hopped back in the van and drove off. I ducked down beneath the window as he passed me and watched him through the rearview mirror until the truck lights disappeared down the Ida Street hillside.

I sat back up in the car seat and stared at Leach's house. It made me sick to think what was going on in there. Sick and sad and philosophical about means and ends. A bad joke that made me laugh.

I checked my watch. It was a quarter past ten. O.K., Harry, I said to myself. Only six or seven more hours and Jellicoe or his wife would be driving back up the street and out would come Junior and the chase would be on in earnest. I sipped some coffee and settled back and waited.

# 24

**THERE WASN'T MUCH** to do for the next six hours.

I sat in the car and stared at the houses along Ida Street and listened to the faint music drifting down the hillside from Celestial. For about half an hour I watched through an attic window a young couple court and spark. She was blonde, in her early twenties, dressed in a peasant skirt and loose white blouse. He was young and fresh-faced, and he already carried himself like a businessman—bowed and brisk and rather officious-looking. They made an odd couple, and they courted politely over a china tea set before lighting candles and settling down on a divan. I don't know what happened after that. I didn't care.

It was love night on the Hill. Hot July weather. The air was sticky and rank with the too-sweet smell of honeysuckle. And I was alone in a car, waiting for

Tracy Leach to finish with his boy lover. While Hugo Cratz was slipping quietly off into death in a hospital bed, dreaming of a girl he had loved. And Jo was dreaming in her Beeker Street apartment of her dead Marine husband and of one Harry Stoner. A detective. Who sat, dreamlessly, in his car, watching the tall yellow street lamps, curved at the tops like feeding giraffes, and the pacific unpeopled street dusted by the tawny lights and rife with the smell of the honeysuckle that flourished along the viaduct. One by one the houses along Ida went dark. The night sounds stopped. And, with them, the occasional laughter of men and women at play. Around three, the music stopped tumbling down the hillside from Celestial. The air grew still and cooler by a decade of degrees. And all that stirred were the branches of the willow tree above my car.

I swallowed tepid coffee and smoked and sang a few songs to myself and waited for the yellow Dodge truck, which didn't come until the night sky had turned violet in the east. At five the keen white beams of the headlights flashed from the north end of the street. They disappeared momentarily as the truck rounded Seasongood Pavillion, then flashed back on as the Dodge entered the stretch of Ida where the park dies away in a grove of pine and the houses start up on the west side, while on the east, where I was parked, the ground rises in a hillock of dense shrubbery and low-hanging willows.

In a few seconds I could hear the sound of the engine and then I could see the truck itself, lazying up the asphalt. The headlights gleamed off the chrome of the cars parked around me. I ducked down again among the styrofoam cups.

Jellicoe stopped in front of Leach's house and sat there, with the motor running. The front blinds opened again, the porch light snapped on—dull yellow in the false dawn. And the little boy came running out of the red door. Jellicoe opened the passenger side door and he crawled in. The truck ground back into gear and started south on Ida, passing me at a slow pace and crossing the viaduct and disappearing down the hillside where Ida drops to the city.

I started the Pinto, pulled out, and U-turned in the street. They were half a mile ahead of me, but I wasn't worried about losing them. Ida is blind down the hillside—just a coil of asphalt carrying through the trees—and the Dodge was going slowly and would be easy to spot on the barren, early-morning streets. I started to feel alive for the first time that night, nervous with excitement as I slid down Ida, through the S-shaped curves, and saw in the distance the big yellow van stopped at a light beneath a trestle in the East Bottoms. I slowed down and pulled to the curb. There was no traffic at all on Front Street and I didn't want Jellicoe to spot me.

I glanced at my watch. It was ten after five.

When the light changed, Jellicoe turned left onto a ramp leading to the parkway. I sped down the hill after him, wheeling through the struts of the L & N trestles and past the smoky warehouses that abut

Front Street to the west and up the ramp onto Columbia Parkway.

Jellicoe continued driving due west on Columbia, past the wall of red brick buildings that is the city's south side, past the stadium, lit green and skeletal across from the downtown buildings. Then he veered south onto I-75, where it feeds the Brent Spence bridge that crosses the Ohio into Covington. I laid back half a mile and followed. A dozen cars and trucks, early birds on their way south, were already on the expressway—formed in a fast-moving pack. It wasn't a crowd, but I managed to lose myself behind a semi, edging out into the fast lane every once in a while to make sure the van was still ahead of me.

We touched down on the Kentucky side. Drove past the dark marts and the deserted auto dealerships and the tall cylinder of the Quality Court Motel, lit in a red band at its topmost floor. And, then up through the sandstone gorge, where the expressway sweeps left and right as it climbs to the flat, bluegrass plain above the river. The highway is divided through those turns by a cement retaining wall, and the wall makes the traffic close and quick and dangerous.

The dawn began in earnest as we topped the gorge, driving the violet and dark blue sky ahead of it. A band of light streaked the eastern horizon and, as the expressway jogged southeast past the mall of the Erlanger Shopping Center, the sun rose bright orange. I flipped down the visor and fished through the glove compartment for a pair of sunglasses—a tricky proposition at close to sixty miles an hour.

Once out of the suburbs the traffic thinned, and we travelled through corn fields turning gold in the sunlight, where farmers on their tractors were already chugging among the tall corn rows. South past hog sties and cow pastures. Under the high-power lines and the concrete overpasses. Through country measured only by mile posts. Decent and featureless as a map.

And, after three-quarters of an hour, with the sun fully up and beginning to warm the air, we stopped.

I saw him pulling off at an exit marked *Belleview*, and I slowed down, letting cars pass me, until he was off the ramp and heading west along a country road. I took the same exit and found myself in the middle of farm land, on an old two-lane highway lined with telephone poles and fenced-in corn rows that bent so close to the roadside that, in some spots, I could have picked an ear from the car window.

The sky was almost fully lighted now. Pale blue and very bright in the rearview mirror. I studied the yellow speck in front of me. Here and there access roads cut through the cornfields and spilled dusty tongues of farm dirt on the highway. About a quarter of an hour up the pike, the yellow van slipped off onto one of those roads and disappeared behind the corn rows.

He'd come to a destination, an ending spot.

Five minutes later, I turned right onto the same

dusty road and jerked to a stop. Yellow dust swirled around the car and settled thickly on the windshield and hood. I cracked a window and dry overheated air flooded through. It must have been a hundred degrees in that field and it was barely seven in the morning. I took a pair of binoculars out of the glove compartment, stepped from the Pinto, and gazed down the road. It continued for a mile or so flanked by the fields, then seemed to fall off abruptly into a gully. The van was parked at the gully's edge and beneath it, in a grove of shade trees, was a white frame farm house with a red tile roof. It was a good-sized house—two rambling floors—with a porch in front and a porch in back. To the north there was a silvery reflection that could have been the beginnings of a creek, and, beyond that, small hills shagged with locust and maple and pine fanned out in a semicircle. The ground in front of the house was grooved like a brain—big yellow grassless whorls of eroded dirt. Behind the house, there was a fenced lawn, with a play-set standing in its center, and a tire hung from a dead oak tree near the fence. A big propane tank was lying on its side next to the rear porch. Nobody was moving around. They'd gone inside to sleep—the Jellicoes and the children who belonged to that play-set.

I put down the binoculars and did some calculation. I couldn't move the car much closer to the house without taking the chance of waking them all up. And walking straight down the road wouldn't do either if someone happened to be looking out a window. I shaded my eyes and searched the corn field. It grew very close to the yard behind the house. If you walk about half a mile down the road, I told myself, and stick close to that corn field, then cut west through the field, you could come out behind the house in that grove of shade trees and make your way through the back yard to the rear porch. What happened after that would depend on the Jellicoes.

I got back in the car and pulled it down about thirty yards and parked it so that it blocked the road. I didn't want anyone making an unexpected entrance or exit. Then I took off my coat and got out. A hot wind blew off the corn field, raising a prickle of sweat on my bare arms. At least the heat felt good on my back. I patted both of my weapons nervously, the way a man pats his coat to make sure he hasn't forgotten his billfold, and started up the dirt road, crouching a little and holding close to the corn row on the west side. A dog barked once, making me jump. But aside from that there wasn't a sound, save for the wind clicking among the shucks.

When I got about two hundred yards from the house, I stepped off the road and into the field. The corn was chest-high and green and smelled of milky sap and of pesticide. I could see clearly over the tops of the rows as I curled through them, frightening birds and field mice and one black, pearly snake. When I got to the grove of oak trees, I ducked behind a gnarled trunk and studied the rear of the house.

It was in surprisingly good shape. The siding was relatively new and freshly painted. The storm windows looked new. There were none of the usual holes or rust spots in the mesh enclosing the porch. It seemed too neat to me, too new. Almost as if it had been built for show. I wondered for whom. Through the wire I could see the kitchen, where sunlight from a front window glared off the tile floors and the aluminum pots and pans hung along a side wall. The kitchen appeared to open on a larger room, perhaps a dining room. It was hard to tell. All of the windows on the second floor were drawn with drapes. The whole house had the clean, righteous look of country life. Currier and Ives. Save that no farmer would still be asleep at seven-thirty in good weather.

There was a grass lawn between me and the rear porch, dotted with children's toys and that sinister jungle gym I'd seen through the binoculars. Fifty feet of open ground. It wasn't going to grow smaller if I just kept looking at it. I slid out from behind the oak, hopped the low wire fence, and ran across the yard.

When I got to the rear porch, I flattened myself against the side of the house. Nobody shrieked or poured burning oil out of the upstairs window. Which was a little disconcerting. When you take pains, you want to feel justified. I had the distinct impression that I could have walked in the front door and nobody would have cared. Either the Jellicoes were incredibly careless, or they felt absolutely safe in their rural hideaway. The lock on the porch door was hook and eye—easy to open with a penknife. I jimmied it quickly and pulled at the handle. The door opened noiselessly and I stepped through onto the planking of the porch. There were a couple of lawn chairs and a chaise on the enclosed porch and a few more toys. I walked through the doorless opening that led to the kitchen.

What I wanted to find was an office or a study—someplace where records might be kept. But I could wander through a lot of rooms and into a lot of trouble before I lucked onto the right one. I thought once about the people I was going to be dealing with and that scared all of the dumb luck philosophy out of my head.

I'd taken some pains to surprise them. It seemed lunatic to blow what little edge I had. I took a deep breath and blew it out and knew that it was better to get the rough part over right away—to put the Jellicoes out of commission and give myself a free hand with the kids and the records, if there were any records.

I looked around the kitchen and decided on a long-handled pot. I didn't want to make too big a racket and bring the whole house down there. Just Lance or Laurie or both of them, at worst.

The kitchen door opened inward and was propped with a rubber stop. Between it and the east wall was a clear space big enough for a man to stand in without being spotted by someone coming through the door. Back to the wall, right arm extended, I would be about two feet from the opening, pointing the pistol chest high on Lance and head high on Laurie. If he came through in a hurry, I might be able to sap him from behind. If he played it cautiously, I'd have no choice but to fire as soon as he peeked around the jamb. There would be no question of missing him at that range. Or of wounding him, either. The bullet would drop him instantly.

I didn't really like it, but at that moment I couldn't see an alternative. Lance was a tough boy. I wasn't sure what I would find outside the kitchen. So it had to be the way I'd imagined. And it had to be in the kitchen. And it had to be soon. I walked over to the pothanger on the north wall, lifted off the long-handled sauce pan, and dropped it to the floor. It clattered and rang against the tile.

I heard a noise overhead. And my heart began to pound.

Someone had gotten out of a bed. I could hear the springs creak and then the pad of footsteps. A male voice said something indecipherable. Another, higher one responded. And then there was a laugh.

That was good. I hoped he'd keep right on laughing all the way to the kitchen.

I backed against the east wall, took the magnum from the shoulder holster, braced my feet against the floorboards, extended my right arm, and pulled back the hammer on the gun.

From the front of the house, I heard a creak of stairs. Then the sound of footsteps got louder and closer. He was coming at a sure, unhurried pace. And before I could take a breath, he was through the door and bending over to pick up the pot. He was naked, hairy on his back. Big, lithe man. With terrific muscles in his arms and thighs. I knew immediately that I wasn't going to be able to sap him—not without both arms. So I took dead aim on his spine and whispered, "Lance."

He didn't move at all for a second. Just stood there, bent over, with the pot in his hand and his back to me. I watched the muscles in his legs. He was taking too long, which meant he was going to charge me. Which meant I was going to kill him where he stood. With a painful effort, I braced my right wrist with my left hand.

"Stand up," I said softly. "Slowly."

His whole body quivered. And his back began to sweat.

He made a deep, violent noise—as if he were expelling all the air inside his huge chest. And very slowly, he stood up.

If he hadn't been naked, I think he would have charged me, whirling madly and bulling into me with all of his strength. But there is nothing quite as vulnerable as a naked body. Lance was human enough to feel that vulnerability for the moment it had taken him to make up his mind.

"Whatchu doin' heah?" he said, without turning around. "What the hell you want?"

"Well, right now, I want you to call Laurie down

here. Sweetly, Lance. Like you were calling her to bed."

"Laurie!" he boomed. "C'mon down heah."

He didn't have much of a bedside manner, Lance. But, then, he wasn't a subtle man. He didn't need to be, with Laurie for a partner.

"Turn around," I said to him. "And go over to that chair and sit down."

He turned. And the look on his big, square, pretty Texas face was purely murderous.

I pointed to a glass breakfast table on the west side of the room. "Sit. And keep it shut, Lance."

He walked over to the table and sat down on a chair.

In a minute I heard Laurie's footsteps. "Hon?" she said sleepily. "What is it?"

Then she came through the door and saw him at the table and I said, "Hello, precious."

"Hello, Harry," she said sweetly. "We thought you were in the hospital." She turned in the doorway and smiled at me.

She was a shameless enough thing. She didn't cover herself. She didn't even blink. She just smiled whitely and stood there, glowing in the sunlight. And she was certainly a voluptuous sight to behold.

"Get over to the table." I waved the gun at her and she stuck out a pouty lip.

"I thought you had more imagination," she said in a hurt little voice. She sashayed to the table. "Tray certainly had his share. We're going to have to have a little talk with him after this is settled." She looked down icily at Lance.

"Jus' shut up," he said to her.

"Now we don't want to wake the little ones," I said. "So let's do this quick. You"—I pointed to Laurie—"get some twine."

She went straight to a drawer by the sink and pulled out a ball of hemp twine. "Now tie him up, Laurie. And I mean *good*. I know you can do it, honey. You've had lots of practice."

She smiled devilishly and went to work on Lance. It was something to see. When she was through, he was hog-tied face down on the floor, his hands stretched behind him and his legs bent at the knees.

"I have a few fillips of my own," she said. "Want me to show you?"

I shook my head. "Gag him."

She took a dish cloth from the sink and gagged Lance with it. When she finished, he looked like a trussed bird.

"Sit down," I told her.

She sat at the table, while I examined the knots. She'd done a good job. It might have fooled someone who couldn't tell a slip from a square. But I'd been in the Boy Scouts, so I knew better. He'd be loose in five minutes, and I'd be dead in six. For some reason that little piece of treachery infuriated me.

I stepped back and kicked Lance hard in the

jaw. His head snapped to the left and fell forward on the tile. A dark blood bruise sprang to his cheek.

As soon as I'd kicked him, Laurie shrieked and bolted for the door. I shot a foot out and tripped her as she went by. She sprawled indecently to the floor.

"My God, my God," she moaned.

"Shut up!" I said viciously.

I walked over and grabbed her by her pretty blonde hair.

"Don't hurt me!" she shrieked again.

"I thought you liked that sort of thing, honey. Clothes pins and darning needles and the sound of some kid in agony."

I pulled her by her hair to her feet. And perhaps, for the first time in ten years, Laurie Jellicoe put an arm across her sweet breasts and a hand in front of her sex and stood, knees shaking and face contorted with terror, like a modest Eve.

I shoved her against the wall and she let out a yelp.

"Now we're going to talk, precious."

She nodded spastically. "Talk."

"I'll skip over the personal stuff. Jones is dead, anyway. What I want to hear you tell me is what happened to Cindy Ann Evans?"

"Preston killed her," she blurted out.

I shook my head and slapped her across the mouth.

Laurie Jellicoe urinated on the floor.

"Let me go to the bathroom," she pleaded. "I'm going to be sick."

"Is that what Cindy Ann said, Laurie? Did she dirty her drawers when you killed her?"

For a second she couldn't catch her breath. "Didn't," she sputtered. "Didn't kill her."

"Who did."

She shuddered and I slapped her again.

"Who did?"

"At the party," she moaned, clutching her belly. "Someone at the party."

"Who?"

"Bascomb. Howie Bascomb."

"The real estate man?"

She nodded. "I'm going to be sick. Please."

"Be sick," I said to her. "Why did you set Preston up?"

Her face grew bright red. She couldn't hold it any longer. And she stooped a little and evacuated on the tile. When she looked back up at me her face was bloated with hatred. And I didn't blame her a bit. But I wasn't about to lay off, either. She deserved it. Maybe not at my hands. But, she deserved it and I was the only one around who knew how much.

"Answer me, Laurie," I said to her. "Or I swear to God I'll make you eat that mess."

"I didn't set him up," she said between her teeth. "We got there after he was dead."

Her eyes glittered like razors. "I'm going to kill you for this. Somehow I'm going to kill you. And it won't be quick. I'll do it like I used to do Cindy Ann. Only *worse*." Her voice throbbed. "So much worse!"

"I believe you would, too.

"Who set Preston up? Who brought the pictures to his apartment?"

She glared at me.

I slapped her again so hard that her nose gushed blood.

But she just glared. The indignity she'd suffered had put iron back in her spine. And I knew that I could kick her around from now till tomorrow and she wouldn't tell me another thing.

I dragged her over to the chair and tied and gagged her. I should have blindfolded her, too. She never stopped glaring at me—torturing me with her eyes. When I'd gotten her tied down good, I retied Lance and left them both in the kitchen while I went house hunting.

Six beautiful children—two boys and four girls—were on the second floor, hiding in a bedroom. They'd heard the fracas downstairs and banded together. They were very frightened, but then they were used to being frightened. Several of them had cigarette burns on their round little tummies and ugly scars on their wrists and ankles. Not one of them was older than sixteen. And they were all rather waif-like and ascetic-looking. Pale, thin, blondish children with the look of refugees.

Eventually I got one of them—the oldest one—to talk to me.

She was Cindy Ann's age. Blonde-haired and

milk-white in the face. With very regular features and large, beautiful green eyes. She had a little swagger about her, where the others were timid and featureless. And her name was Cissy Hill.

Cissy spoke with a nasal Kentucky twang. She had no parents, she told me. All the children were parentless. And, unbelievable as it sounded, that clean white farm house was licensed by the Commonwealth as a halfway house for homeless children. Which helped explain the new paint.

"We ain't orphans exactly. We had folks. All of us but Becky. But they done died or got killed like mine in an auto crash. When we went on the state, they sent us here. It ain't half bad, 'cept when Laurie gets riled. Then it's bad. The rest of the time it's mostly fun. Hell, I was gettin' poked 'fore I was thirteen. Don't make me no never mind whether I do't for fun or for Laurie and Lance. We get to dress up nice."

I asked her to show me the rest of the house.

And she smiled cunningly. "You mean where they keep the pictures, don't you."

I said that was exactly what I meant.

She said O.K., but warned me to lock the rest of the kids in the bedroom or they'd go downstairs to be with Lance and Laurie. So I locked the five of them in the bedroom and followed Cissy downstairs and down a hall to a paneled room, hung with photos of Laurie and furnished with black vinyl furniture. There was a desk on the east wall. Cissy walked over to it and said, "In there. But it's locked."

I tried the handle on the file drawer. It wouldn't budge. So I told Cissy to stand back and she said, "Oh, good. You're going to shoot it!"

And I did shoot it with the magnum.

The gun made a terrific roar and the desk drawer exploded.

"Far out!" Cissy said.

I walked back over and pulled out what was left of the drawer. It was filled with pictures and several tins of eight millimeter film and a fat black address book stocked with names and notes. All of the stuff that the Jellicoes held over the heads of their clients. It was a perfect haul that would put them out of business and behind bars. I asked Cissy to find me a bag. She got one out of a closet and I dropped all the evidence into it. And then we sat down on the black vinyl couch, with Laurie Jellicoe peering down at us from every wall, and had our chat about Cindy Ann.

"Were you at the party the night she was killed?" I asked her.

Cissy got a sad look on her face and said, "Oh, yes. It was awful."

"How did it happen?"

"I ain't for sure, exactly. They was in a different room from us, and it was real late. And we heard this explosion, like when you shot the desk. Then Lance come out all upset. And Laurie kept talking to him, trying to calm him down. He didn't like what happened none. He's always been a soft touch. But she sure ain't. I ain't for sure what happened. I liked Cindy Ann. She was 'bout my age, you know. And some of them others is just kids." She was older than the others and, in a few years, those beautiful green eyes would become lively green predators in a predatory world. She caught me studying her and smiled raffishly. "They made us leave real quick after that explosion. And I ain't seen Cindy Ann since then."

I stared at the desk and thought, suddenly, that I would never know. Not if this eager girl couldn't tell me. That Hugo's darling might as well be drowned in the river. So lost was she from the world. Buried, burned. Gotten rid of after the embarrassment of her death—after some drunken realtor had killed her for fun or in rage—by the Jellicoes or their silent friend.

"Does anybody else come out here and talk with the Jellicoes?" I asked Cissy.

"Aw, him," she said disgustedly. "He's just a dumb old cracker."

"Who?"

"That man. He come out here with a mean nigger once and awhile. Most times just the nigger comes out. He stays with us while Lance and Laurie ain't around. That old cracker don't like Lance much. He talks to Laurie mostly."

"What's he look like?"

"Just an old man. With glasses."

"O.K., Cissy. I guess that's it."

She looked at me curiously. "What's going to happen to us, mister? What you going to do?"

"I'm going to call the police," I said. "And see that they get you to some decent homes."

"Aw, shucks," she said morosely. "I was afraid of that. There goes all our fun."

I laughed at her. "You'll still have fun, Cissy. There's lots of girls and boys your age at high schools."

"They may be my age. But they ain't *lived*."

"You can teach them."

"Hey!" she said, brightening. "That's a thought!"

There was a phone on the desk. I picked it up and called the Highway Patrol. The local cops would probably have been thoroughly bribed. Judging from what Leach had said about the clientele at the Jellicoes' party, I wasn't even sure that the state troopers were safe. Just to be sure, I called the F.B.I., too. I told them both where I was—about six miles west on the Belleview road. And told them a little of the situation. They said they'd dispatch cars right away. And then I went out to the kitchen to check on Lance and Laurie.

He'd come around a little. And she was still sitting there, murdering me in her mind.

Cissy peeked through the door and said, "What a smell!"

At ten A.M., the highway patrol arrived. And ten minutes later a khaki-colored government car pulled up outside the farm house. After a few minutes of hassling about jurisdictions, the cops joined hands and began the long process of legal action against Lance and Laurie Jellicoe.

# 25

I WAS IN the Highway Patrol station at Belleville
for three hours, explaining my part in the business.
The kids, especially Cissy, were eager to cooperate.
And, soon, they had a whole bank of stenographers
working double time. It was a very ugly bust, and it
had statewide ramifications. Someone had certified
the Jellicoes to house wards of the court and someone had been sending selected children to them.
Disentangling the mess was a job for the federal district attorney and for the attorney general at Frankfort. By two in the afternoon, the little office was
buzzing with prosecutors and special investigators
from the capital.

"Boy, to look at 'em, it sure is hard to believe,"
one of the troopers said to me.

I nodded. "They're a handsome pair."

The last time I saw the Jellicoes, they were being

loaded into a station wagon. Lance's jaw was bruised and swollen and Laurie had a split lip, but, outside of that, they were indeed a handsome pair. They held their manacled hands in front of their faces when the photographers started shooting. Then a deputy stepped in and whisked them away.

Cissy, who had developed a mild crush on me, started to cry. "Damn!" she said. "There goes the easy life."

"Buck up, honey," I told her. "You'll be better off without them."

At three some agents from the Juvenile Court came to pick up the children. And as they were rounding them up, Cissy ran up, threw her arms around my neck, and gave me a sultry kiss goodbye. It made me sad to think that she would probably never know how wrong that kiss had been.

"Goodbye, honey," she said cheerfully. "I'm off to the work farm."

"Take care, Cissy."

"I shall," she said. She started to walk away, then turned back. "I thought of something I meant to tell you at the house. You know that man you was asking me about—the one that come to see Laurie and Lance fairly regular?"

"Yeah," I said.

"Well, I don't remember his face none. But I *do* remember that car." She got a dreamy look in her eye. "It was a Cad-*ee*-lac," she said lovingly. "A pink Cad-*ee*-lac. And it had the funniest thing on the hood!"

I shivered up and down my spine. "Bull's horns."

"Sure enough," she said with surprise. "How'd y'all know that?"

"A lucky guess."

"Yeah." She looked at me oddly, then a smile broke across her face. "Goodbye, Harry. Someday I'll come see you. You can count on that."

———

There was a pay phone in the hall of the Highway Patrol building. I got a couple of dimes out of my trousers, sat down in the booth, and closed the folding door. A little fan went on overhead with a whisper. I just sat there for about five minutes, juggling the coins until they were warm from my palm and thinking about Red Bannion—an ordinary old man with glasses and a pink Cadillac.

It made perfect sense that it would have been him. He had the connections throughout the state to set the Jellicoes up in business and to keep the local police away from the farm. And it had been Red Bannion who had touted me onto Preston La-Forge, when I started asking questions about Cindy Ann. And, if Laurie could be trusted at all, it had also been Red Bannion who had driven up to Preston's house—in the heart of that storm—and frightened him into committing suicide.

It did make sense.

That's why Lance had been upset the night of the suicide. Preston's death truly *hadn't* been his doing. Perhaps, at that point, he didn't know what had happened. Perhaps, Laurie didn't either. But she had learned by the following night—when she met me at the Busy Bee. And she'd kept me occupied with drinks and small talk, while Abel Jones searched the apartment and prepared to murder me. That had probably been Red's idea, too. He'd seen three of the pictures. He wanted to see them all. And Abel Jones was just the man to jump at the chance to do Red Bannion a favor.

Good old Red, who only wanted to be a help.

Well, he had warned me off, in a way. Although he must have known I'd go after LaForge. In fact, he'd probably wanted me to. Preston panics and kills himself. Cindy Ann's death is accounted for. The Jellicoes go on with business as usual. And nobody ever has to be the wiser. Escorts Unlimited must have been a sweet and profitable enterprise to make a man like Bannion take so many chances to protect it. But, then, to keep Howie Bascomb—who owned half of the Riverside Mall—in your back pocket, along with most of the officials in Boone and Franklin counties, you'd be willing to take risks.

I juggled the coins and listened to the fan blades whirring through the hot enclosed air. There was no way around it. Sooner or later I was going to have to ask myself just how big a part Porky Simlab had played in Red's scam. On the surface, the Jellicoes' operation seemed as far from Charles Street as you could get. But then, on the surface, Red Bannion had seemed a tough and earnest old man, eager to put some unsavory characters out of business.

Well, I owed Porky something after ten years. And what it came down to was the benefit of the doubt. I don't have that many loyalties in my life—if loyalty was the right word for what I felt for that seedy, amiable old hoodlum with his cracker barrel speech and winking mouth. But after what I'd done that morning to Lance and Laurie Jellicoe, after what had happened the night before between Jo and me, after seeing Hugo being wheeled to the grave, I felt the need to show some loyalty to someone. Just to reestablish my own sense of myself as a decent man. Or as a sentimental fool. Sometimes I can't tell the difference.

I slipped the coins in the phone slot and dialed the Charles Street house. If Porky *could* be kept out of it, I'd do my part. I wouldn't bring the state police down on his greasy old head until I knew for sure just where he fit in.

Bannion answered almost immediately. "Yessuh?" he said. "Red Bannion heah."

"This is Harry, Red."

"Harry, boy," he said warmly. "We heard some rumor y'all got shot at last night. T'aint true, is it, son? I done warned you about them fellas."

"Yeah. You sure did."

"What's wrong, son?" He was a quick old man. He'd heard right through my voice to the heart of it.

"I *know*, Red," I said wearily. "I know all about

the Jellicoes and the farm outside Belleville. I know
about Preston. And I know what happened to Cindy
Ann."

"I see," he said.

"Why, Red? Why'd you do it?"

"Aw, hell, son. For the money. Why else?"

I sighed heavily. "I'm going to go to the police,
Red. I just figured I owed you the courtesy of a
call."

"Well, you go on right ahead, son. Do what you
think is best."

That bothered me. "You don't care?"

He made that sound again—that plaintive
"hem."

"I ain't going to jail, son. I know too many people for that. I ain't sayin' that you couldn't be a
bother. No sir, I ain't sayin' that at all. You know a
good deal 'bout my affairs. And I ain't sure who all
you done already told. But, son, I been hanging
round courthouses most of my life and you may
bring the law down on me, but they ain't going to be
able to prove a thing. That girl, for example. Don't
have to be no lawyer to know that without a body
there ain't no crime."

"Where is it, Red? Where did you stash her?"

He snorted merrily. "Hell, son, I tell you that
and we wouldn't have nothing to discuss. I'm a gam-
bler, Harry. I been one most of my life. You want to
find out what happened to Cindy Ann, you come to
me. But I got to warn you, son. You best come *prepared*." Something calm and wintry filtered into

**273**

Red's voice like that blue snow that Preston had seen falling on those beautiful children. "Might be better that way. Just you and me. I ain't got no hankering to see this drag through the courts. I ain't got that much time left. You want to know about that girl, you meet me at Willie Keeler's theater in about an hour."

I didn't say anything.

"It's a slim chance, son. I ain't really offering you nothing but a shot at me—head-on. And, of course, a chance of finding out what's left of that girl. If I was you, I'd turn me down. But, then, I'm not you."

He hung up.

═════

I hadn't had any sleep in some thirty hours, and I was feeling too fuzzy to drive. I popped the bennies at a water fountain beside the phone booth. Then sat down on a wood bench and waited for the rush. In ten minutes, I was rarin' to go again. I checked out with the desk sergeant and walked through the station house door into the clean blue afternoon. The Pinto was parked in a gravel lot beside the station. I climbed in, spun my wheels in the loose rock, kicked up a little white dust, and, in a minute, I was back on the expressway, heading north.

I thought about Red Bannion as I breezed along the highway. He was going to try to kill me. That much was sure. But not until he knew how much I knew and whom I'd told it to. That's the only way I

could account for this recklessness. As for my own
. . . maybe it was the bennies, but I had the strange
feeling that I was driving through that bright beautiful afternoon to participate in an old-fashioned
drama of justice and revenge. I was a little drunk on
the absurdity of it. A gunfight in front of the shoe
stores and liquor stores and dry cleaners of North
Main Street. Just like the old Golden Deer days,
when Red had been chief of police and Seventh
Street had echoed with gunfire. It tickled some dark
spot inside me to think of it. And I had to make
myself calm down and relax. Remind myself that
meeting him face-to-face was probably the only way
to settle this business. Scare up sanity like a ghost, to
mask the insane excitement—the vicious need to
know what had become of the girl and to seek revenge for it. And for myself, too. Because he'll get
away, Harry, that little man was whispering in my
ear. He'll get away, just as he said he would. Bribe a
judge, pack a jury. And go free. After all the blood-
shed and the death. He'd go free. And that was an
imperfection that little man couldn't abide. A crack
in the damn world.

I shivered and told myself I was talking sense,
while the countryside whirled past me in a dream.

The sun was well beyond meridian as I slalomed
through those S-shaped turns, where the expressway dipped down to the river through that dry sul-
fur-yellow gorge. On my right, the Quality Court
Motel was blazing in the sun, like a pillar of fire, and
all those stores and auto lots that had been dead

shadows in the early morning were filled with color and life. I zipped by them and up onto Brent Spence, where the tires sang on the roadbed. Across the muddy Ohio with its half dozen coal barges pushed by white-capped tugs. And back to the city. Then up Columbia a mile or so to the suspension bridge and back across the river to the sleepy hamlet of Newport.

The day was vivid and crystal clear. One of those rare summer days when the smog is washed down river by a hot wind and, suddenly, you can see—numbers and lettering and the texture of skin. Like getting a new pair of eyes. The Pinto dipped down again, past the concrete ponds where hundreds of cars sparkled in the sunlight, through the shady streets with their worn and suffering houses, and out to Main, down that avenue that's lined for half a mile with flat, glassy, unattractive shops. And, then I could see the marquee of Keeler's theater, lit faintly by soft yellow bulbs, and the big pink Cadillac parked in front of it, with lean, bullet-headed Red Bannion propping himself against it and gazing sedately at the street. I pulled in behind him and parked. I was full of unhealthy excitement as I stepped out the door, and I could feel both of the guns weighing against my body as if they were the only things I had on.

Red had a tin of film in his right hand, and he waved with it to me and pointed to the theater lobby. I took a very close look at the cars parked along the street and across from the theater and began to feel some of the danger I had placed myself in. But it was too late to start acting sanely. I took a deep breath and followed Bannion into the lobby.

It was cold inside the theater. And dimly-lighted. It took me a few seconds to adjust to the dark.

Willie Keeler wasn't anywhere around. And that worried me.

The only other person in the lobby was a rough-looking kid, sitting on a stool behind the candy counter. He had a blue usher's cap on his head and a bored, vicious look on his face.

Bannion didn't look at him as he passed by the counter and through the door marked "Office." He sat down behind Keeler's desk and folded his hands at his lips.

"Shut the door behind you, will you, Harry?"

I closed it and he pointed to a chair in front of the desk. I sat.

He studied me for a moment, his hands folded at his lips. Try as I could, I couldn't make anything out of that look. It was the same weary, small town cop's face, with its cold, dispassionate eyes, magnified slightly by the lenses of his glasses. And the same bland clothes—the same loamy brown leisure suit and flat, tieless white shirt that Porky wore. Sitting there scratching his upper lip with one finger and eyeing me expressionlessly, he looked exactly like the shrewd old cop that he was.

"So," he said after a time. "We got a problem."

"No, Red. You've got a problem."

"Well, I guess I seen some trouble in my life. I'll get by."

"Not this time," I said coldly.

"Maybe not." He sat up in the chair and pushed the tin of film over to me. "There she is."

"Who?"

"That damn girl. That damn Cindy Ann."

I looked at the aluminum can and then back at Red.

He sat back in the desk chair and stared dully at the desktop. "You know, you can figure and you can figure. Cover 'bout every angle there is. Then some jackass comes along with one you never heard of and it all goes to hell. I didn't want that girl dead. Last thing in the world I needed. But some no-account fool with too much liquor in his fat, silly gut goes a little crazy one night. And . . ." He slapped the edge of the desk with his fingertips. "There you are."

Red unscrewed the can of film. There was a viewer on Keeler's desk, probably what he used to preview the loops for the quarter machines. Red patted the reel of film into his palm, slipped it on one of the arms of the viewer, and fed it through to the take-up reel. He flipped a switch on the housing, and the prism lit up.

It was hard to see what was going on at first. Whoever had been holding the camera had been doing a very bad job. The lens jumped around the room from face to face until it finally settled on the bed.

And there she was. Hugo's Cindy Ann. Preston
LaForge was on top of her, and for a few seconds he
obscured her body. All you could see was his naked
back and her white legs stretched out on either side
of his buttocks. LaForge began to pump faster—the
speed of his movements exaggerated by the speed
of the film. And then he stopped moving, arched his
back, and pushed up from the bed with his arms.
You could see Cindy Ann's pale face again beneath
his chest. It was twisted with pleasure. Her little
mouth opened in a silent "Oh," then the film went
blank for a second where it had been spliced.

The prism filled again with the bed, this time
from a closer vantage. Cindy Ann was sitting up on
it, her back to the headboard, and you could see her
naked torso from the forehead to a little below the
hips. She had a vibrator between her legs and, from
time to time, she would press her knees together
luxuriously and make a silent groan. Someone got
in the way of the lens momentarily, then backed out
of the picture. Cindy's face had grown rapt. She
tossed her head from side to side, moving the vibrator with her hands and licking her pale lips. She was
trembling on the edge of orgasm and you could see
the pale flesh of her chest grow mottled and her red
hair—dark in the black and white film—sway like it
was seaborne about her face. Just as she was about
to come—her eyes squeezed closed, her mouth
opened in noiseless wail—someone put a pistol to
her head and pulled the trigger.

The right side of Cindy Ann's skull exploded in

blood and she fell out of the frame. There were arms and frightened faces, the camera jerked around; then the prism went bright with light.

Red took a deep breath and clicked off the viewer. The motor whined down and the leader stopped slapping against the prism housing.

When I looked up from the prism, I saw the gun in his hand.

"Harry, y'all got to believe me. I didn't want that to happen."

"Sure," I said. And my voice sounded as if it were coming from another world. "What I got to do is kill you, Red."

"I was afraid you'd take that point of view. I guess I would, too. If I was in your shoes."

"You could have taken care of the sick, twisted bastard that did that," I said. "You could have done that much, Red."

He sighed. "I wanted to. You can believe that. But he's a powerful man, Harry. And I guess I just couldn't bring myself to kill the goose. Not over a kid like her."

I surged out of the chair and lunged at the pistol.

But he moved with terrific quickness and slammed the revolver barrel across my cheek.

"Don't try that again, son," he said grimly. "I'll blow your face off if you do."

He'd split my cheek wide open with the gun. I could feel the blood pouring down it. Red pulled a handkerchief from his pocket and tossed it over to me.

"You better staunch that."

I pressed it to my cheek and glared at him. "Now, what?"

"We're going for a ride, Harry."

He stood up behind the desk. "Y'all pull that gun from your belt and toss it on the desk. Gently now, son. With two fingers, like y'all was at a lady's tea."

I pulled the gun out and dropped it on the desk.

"Now the one under your shoulder, Harry. Same way."

I pulled out the magnum.

"Nice weapon," Bannion said. "Now, here's how it's going to be, son. We're going to walk out to the car. You try anything, I'll kill you. It don't make no difference to me, now, whether I get seen or not. I'll come out of it one way or t'other. Y'all understand what I'm saying?"

I nodded.

"Good." He collected the can of film and slipped it in his pocket. "Now move it."

I opened the office door and we walked out into the lobby.

Red nodded at the usher. "There's some guns in there, son. Y'all want to collect them for us?"

"You want some help with him?" the kid said.

"I don't think so," Red said gently.

# 26

THERE WAS A driver sitting in the front seat of the Cadillac when we walked back out into the glare of Main Street. He was high yellow with a wispy black goatee on his chin, big yellow wolfish teeth, and the high puffed cheeks of the ex-boxer. He hadn't been hard to hit in his prime—that one—but he'd been hard to put down. There was scar tissue over both of his eyes, and his left ear was badly deformed, like someone had hung a barbell from the lobe when he was a child. He was wearing a knit skull cap on his head, a white T-shirt, and yellow rayon slacks with a scarlet bunting down either leg. He smelled of sweat and whiskey, and he looked at me, as Red pushed me into the back seat, with a kind of savage anticipation—the way a cannibal must size up a prospective meal.

"This heah's Rafe," Red said, getting in beside

me. "You going to be seein' a lot of him, Harry."
Red reached into a coat pocket and pulled out a pair
of handcuffs. "Hold out your hands, son."

When I hesitated, he gave me a good hard shot
on the right arm with the gun barrel.

"That's better," he said, cuffing me.

He pointed with the gun to Rafe, who started the
car up and pulled out onto Main. We were heading
south, into the farmland.

"Let me tell you a little story about Rafe, yon-
der," Red said, settling back on the seat. "He used
to be a boxer. Golden Gloves. He had him some
professional bouts, too. Didn't you, son?"

The back of Rafe's head went up and down.
"Yessuh," he said softly.

"Rafe don't like white boys none. One of them
killed his brother. Ain't that right, Rafe?"

"Yessuh," he said.

"Cut his throat up in Lima, when the boy didn't
have but six months left to serve. I helped him out a
bit with funeral expenses and such. But that didn't
change nothing about the way Rafe feels. Son—the
last white boy I turned over to him took twelve
whole hours in dying. Probably would've taken
longer, only Rafe bled him so much there just wasn't
anything left for his poor heart to pump. You ever
seen a man die, Harry? I don't mean quick. I mean
slow. Razor cuts and burns from a solderin' iron.
Why towards the end, they just go sleepy with the
pain of it. They take a look at what's become of 'em,
and they just don't care anymore."

"Is that how you got to Preston? Threatening him with Rafe?"

Bannion laughed. "Hell, no. All we had to do with that fairy was show him a few pictures. A bit of splicin' in that movie made it look like he done fucked her and killed her all by hisself. Weren't no question in my mind when I left him what he'd do. But I did have Rafe waitin' around—just in case."

We passed a sign marking the city limit and kept heading south, through a hilly section green with blue grass and pine. Then the road curved up out of the river bottoms, past old Beverly Hills, and leveled out. Shops began to appear at half-mile intervals— little roadside cafes and two-pump gas stations with junk autos in their lots. And, then, we broke free of town life entirely. Huge tobacco fields, tented for acres with gauze canopies, filled either side of the road.

"Lookie there." Red pointed out the window.

A farmer was burning off the stubble in a corn field, and the late afternoon sky was filled with black, corn-sweet smoke.

"I should never have left that," Red said wistfully. "But, hell, it was depression and a man has to eat. And, then, Porky's always done right by me." He looked out the window at the wind-blown smoke and sighed. "It sure ain't been my day, has it, son?" He looked over at me. "You busted the Jellicoes, didn't you?"

I didn't say anything.

"Sure you did," Red said, hefting the gun in his

hands as if he were testing its weight. "You're a good young cop, son. I always liked you." He jiggled the gun for a moment. "I'm going to try to make it easy for you, Harry. You got to die. There ain't no discussin' that. But, it don't have to be Rafe's way."

It was the old Ike and Mike act—the good cop and the tough one. Only he was doing it all by himself. He'd never really stopped being a cop—Bannion. Maybe it'd been the only thing he'd ever worked at with talent and pride.

"I need to know a few things, Harry," he said gently. "I need to know how far you done gone in this business. It may not seem like much I'm offerin', son. But, 'bout noon tomorrow, you're going to see it a mighty different way. You think on't, heah?"

He sat back on the seat and stared through the front windshield with a watery eye. He was actually crying, so moved had he been by his own account of the hopelessness of my situation.

I laughed out loud.

Bannion took a pair of sunglasses out of his pocket and flipped them on, pocketing the horn-rims with his right hand. He licked his lips and stared through the dark green glasses at the open road.

———

It must have been close to seven when we pulled off the highway. The sun was setting above the tree-tops in the west, and we headed into it, down a paved side road into a cool green dell of oak and maple. The trees were thick on the hillsides—so thick I thought we must have entered a park or a preserve. It was virtually night in the woodland— the sun just a red glow on the tree-capped shoulder of the hills. Rafe flipped on the headlights and turned left off the road onto a gravel lane that carried back into the woods. We followed the lane for half a mile until the headlights bounced off the windowpanes of a small cabin tucked among the trees. It was a weathered plank hunting lodge, set up on stilts, with a pitch roof overhanging a railed porch. It looked as if it hadn't been visited in many years.

"We're there." Red tapped Rafe on the shoulder.

Rafe cut the engine, and a dead, woodsy silence filled the car.

"Quiet, ain't it?" Bannion said.

He got out of the car, walked around to my side, and opened the door.

"Git on out, Harry."

Rafe got out, too, and stretched his long, muscular arms.

I took a quick look around.

There was a stone wall on the west side of the cabin. To the east, the forest grew to within ten feet of the cabin wall. The ground behind the lodge seemed to fall away abruptly. There were some stone steps set in the earth where it plunged downward. I estimated we were about seventy miles southwest of Newport, on a private estate about halfway between Cincinnati and Louisville.

Red pushed me toward the cabin. "Git on up there," he said.

My shoulder had been aching dully for better than two hours, and my face stung where Red had gashed it with the gun barrel. But I was just too tired to care. I trudged up the path to the cabin and up four steps to the porch and stood there waiting for Bannion and Rafe.

In an hour or so, I'd be dead—if I was lucky.

It wasn't that I wasn't afraid of it. I was. But I was more disgusted with myself than I was afraid. And angrier than I was disgusted. If I hadn't been so cocksure, three hours before, that Bannion was as much of a loner at heart as I was, I wouldn't have been standing on that porch. I would have been standing on Porky's porch on Charles Street, trying to explain why the highway patrolmen were interrupting his barbecue.

Red Bannion hadn't turned out to be a bit sentimental where it really cost him. He had a cop's mind, pure and simple. For him it would always be a question of the right tool for the job. And there wasn't going to be any shoot-out, any last minute drama of justice and revenge. If I hadn't been so damn coy and self-involved—so set on finishing it off on my own—I would have know it immediately, as soon as I walked into that theater and saw the tough kid behind the candy counter. The only thing I couldn't understand was why he'd dragged me seventy miles into the woods before pulling the trigger.

"Why are we here, Red?" I asked him.

"You wanted to find that girl, didn't you?" he said archly. "Well, there's a lime pit down back aways. That's where she's lying. That's where you'll be lying, too, Harry. They say it's supposed to comfort a man to know where his bones will rest."

He pushed the cabin door open and pulled me through.

There was a trestle table inside the cabin, two wood chairs, a fireplace on the south wall facing the door, open rafters overhead, and dust and cobwebs everywhere else. Even the windows were coated with dirt.

Red lit a hurricane lamp and set it on the table.

"Start a fire, Rafe."

The black walked back out the door to gather kindling. Red sat down on a chair by the table and looked up at me through those dark green sunglasses. It looked like he had two hurricane lamps for eyes.

"Well, son, looks like the end of the road. You ain't had a long life, but it's been a lively one."

"I'm not dead, yet, Red," I said to him.

"Yes, you are. You just don't know it yet."

He tilted back on the chair and hefted the gun in his hands.

I thought a second about rushing him. Now would be the time, while Rafe was outside. The room was about thirty feet square and he was in the middle of it. From where I was standing by the door, it would take me three strides to reach him and pitch him to the floor. Give him a second to react. And I'd just be on top of him when the first slug exploded through my belly. He wouldn't be able to get the barrel up much higher than that in a second. Hell, he wouldn't have to.

"You're welcome to try, son," Red said and grinned. "I would, too, if I was in your shoes."

"If I were in your shoes, you'd be dead."

"Why in hell'd you do it, son? That's what I can't figure. Why'd you go down to the theater? You must've known I wasn't going to let you leave." He grinned again, his teeth yellow in the lamp light. "But, then, you figured you could take a sixty-year-old man, didn't you?" He laughed spitefully. "You're a fool, son. Getting yourself killed for a half-witted old man and a girl that didn't have the sense of a hog. Porky'd be plumb ashamed of you."

I had to try something. And soon. So I said, "Porky already knows," and watched his reaction.

I couldn't have been entirely wrong about Bannion. Even small town cops have a parochial sense of honor, a small spot of sentimentality. And I was guessing that Porky was smack in the center of Red's conscience. I was also guessing that Porky wasn't a part of Red's scam, and that Red didn't want him to know how he'd been moonlighting. I guessed right, because Bannion clicked down on the chair and peered at me over the rims of his glasses.

"You're lying," he said in a tough, steady voice.

I leaned back against the wall. "Right after I got

through with the Jellicoes, Red. He knows all about you."

Bannion juggled the gun. "Rafe!" he shouted.

A second later, the black bounded through the door.

"Take this son-of-a-bitch out back and kill him. I'm going back to town."

"Yessuh," he said. "Whatchu want me to do with the body?"

"In the lime pit, Rafe. I'll be back out here to-morrow, early."

He started for the door. "Work him over a little, Rafe, before you shoot him," he said over his shoulder. "That boy needs to be taught to respect his elders 'fore he dies."

He stepped out the door and off the porch. And, in a minute, the woodland silence was broken by the sound of the engine.

Rafe watched me while the sound of the car faded through the trees. His face was dull-eyed and vicious and I could see the muscles in his forearms flexing a little. He had a pistol tucked in his belt. I looked down at it, and he smiled.

"Why don' you try?" he said impartially. "You big enough."

I showed him the cuffs.

He shook his head. "Not yet. Git over to the ta-ble."

I walked over and sat down.

"You wanna drink, maybe?" He walked over to a carton in the corner beside the door and fished a bottle out of it. Rafe moved with a boxer's rolling gait. He bounced on his feet and strutted in front of me. He was enjoying it—making me wait until he was ready. He cracked the seal on the whiskey bottle, tilted it to his lips, and took a long drink. His dull brown eyes never left me for a second.

Like most old boxers, Rafe had something soft and childlike in his face. I was hoping it was stupidity and not simply scar tissue. He didn't move stupidly, that was sure. He was quick and lithe and agile. One of those rare men who are absolutely confident about their bodies. He was about my height, maybe ten or fifteen pounds heavier.

He had a gold tooth in the back of his mouth and, when he smiled suddenly—his thick yellow lips opening in animal rictus and his fat yellow nose splaying against his cheeks—it glittered in the lamp light. Rafe dangled the bottle at his side, walked over to my chair and, in one swift movement, broke the bottle across the back of my skull.

I fell out of the chair to the floor, and he kicked me hard in the chest.

I didn't know where to try to reach first. I could feel the glass shards in my scalp, and my chest was burning. I doubled up in the fetal position. He walked around me a few times, kicking me at his leisure. Hard, swift kicks. When he got to my groin, I passed out.

When I came out of it, I was still on the floor, curled up like a baby. It was late. I could hear the night humming outside the cabin windows.

He'd built a fire in the chimney and the room flickered in the firelight. He'd turned the hurricane lamp down. It was glowing softly on the table.

I wet my lips. They worked.

It's hard to describe what the rest of me felt like. There might have been a spot or two on my torso that didn't burn with a bruise. I couldn't tell. I'd been worked over before, but this was the worst I'd taken. I ached inside and out. And I knew, at once, that I couldn't take any more—that if he slugged me again I would hemorrhage all to hell on the inside and drown in my own blood. It hurt to take a breath.

"I see you comin' around."

He was sitting at the table above me. There was another bottle in his hand. Something bright and terrifying was glittering beside the lamp.

I tried to roll over and groaned.

"H'm," he said. "That was jus' round one, honey. Y'all goin' to hate round two."

He stood over me and grabbed me by the handcuffs and dragged me to the second chair, which he'd set across from his at the table.

"Git up!" he roared and yanked me to my feet.

For a second, I thought I was going to pass out again. He plopped me on the chair and sat down across from me.

He picked up the razor and teased it with his thumb.

"Please," I said. "Shoot me."

He laughed—a truly terrifying laugh and stared madly at my face.

"No, honey. That's round three."

"Why?" I swallowed some blood and made my eyes focus on him.

"Like the man said, I don't like you. When I was in 'Nam, had me a boy like you in the outfit. Man you should have seen what I did to that po' soul."

"What outfit?" I said stupidly.

"LURPs," he said. "Y'all in 'Nam?"

I nodded.

He leaned back and gazed at me. "Maybe we skip round two," he said.

I had gotten a bit of body sense back. I knew which way I was facing. And I could move my right arm. Given another few minutes, I could stand. I wanted those minutes.

"I was with a Cav patrol got wiped out in Ia Drang valley," he said. "You go back that far?"

"'65," I said.

"That's it!" He slapped the table. "Charley killed every last soul in my outfit, 'cept _me_. Had to hide under the bodies whilst they stuck 'em to make sure we was dead." I looked over at his face. It was mournful and remote. "Some'n happen to me after that. My mind ain't never been right since then. Then when Tommy got hisself killed." He looked up at me. "Man, you a mess."

"I feel like a mess."

"I ain't goin' to whittle on you none. You had you beating. Kin you walk?"

I could, now. But I could never run. Whatever I tried, I'd have to try it in that room. And quickly. "No," I said.

"Take you a swig of this."

He picked up the bottle and I flinched.

Rafe laughed heartily. "I ain't goin' to hurt you no more. Go ahead. Drink."

I showed him the handcuffs and he dug in his pocket for the key. "Goin' to be all right," he said, unlocking the cuffs. He held out the bottle again, and I reached for it shakily. He was directly in front of me. The hurricane lamp was a foot to my right. There was nothing else on the table. He'd pocketed the razor.

I took the bottle by the neck and started carrying it toward my lips. He was watching me, one arm on the table, urging me with his eyes.

"Go on," he said, leaning forward a bit.

I brought the bottle up to my lips, then jabbed it straight back in a stabbing motion, right into Rafe's forehead.

It broke instantly and Rafe shouted, "Jesus!" as the blood sprang out.

He grabbed his head, red with blood and whiskey. And I lunged for the lamp, burning my hands on the glass chimney, and sent it hurtling into his face. It shattered in my hands, and then Rafe's face just exploded in flame.

He threw himself backward off the chair, shrieking, and rolled across the floor, clawing at his flesh.
His T-shirt had started up, too. And, for half a minute, his whole upper body was jacketed in blue alco-
hol fire.

I would have helped him if I could have. But it
took me over a minute to get to my feet; and, by
then, he'd stopped shrieking and skittering across
the floor like a dying moth and was lying on his back
about ten feet from the table, his knees up and his
arms spread on the floor. One side of his face looked
like bubbling brown sugar, and there were smoking
patches of charred flesh on his chest, his arms and
his belly. The smell was hellish.

I was leaning on the table—barely standing.

Rafe was on the floor—lying still.

And then, he got up.

The dead, smouldering son-of-a-bitch got up!

At first I couldn't believe it—watching him turn
and heave and groan and lift again, pushing himself
off the floor as if he were doing a push-up with one
blackened arm. I screamed when I saw him half-
standing. And, with a strength born of sheer terror,
I grabbed the chair beside me and swung it at his
head.

It caught him across his chest and he crashed to
the floor, as if he'd gone down on wet ice. I pounced
on him and dug the pistol from his belt and held
it to his head and pulled the trigger. The gun
snapped viciously, and Rafe's head cracked like an
egg. A gurgle of trapped gas came from his throat.

I pawed and lunged my way back to the table. And just sat there, gun pointed at his corpse, waiting for him to get up again. I just couldn't believe he was dead—on the floor of that nightmarish cabin, flickering with red firelight. I must have held the gun on him for twenty minutes before I realized that, this time, he wasn't going to get back on his feet.

# 27

THERE WAS A third bottle of whiskey in that carton beside the door. And that's how I spent the rest of the night, drinking at the table in the dying firelight and dreaming, eyes open, of Rafe, as his face exploded in flame—exploded like a wad of crumpled newspaper, fattening with it, feeding on it as if it were something black and rich and bloating. The smell in the cabin was horrible. And the only reason I didn't go outside until first light was that I couldn't move my legs again until first light and, then, only with stomach-turning pain. I went outside on the porch and threw up.

I sat there on the railing—one hand against the house to steady me and the other crooked around the whiskey bottle—and watched it grow light in the east. It's Thursday, I told myself. I looked at my watch. It's Thursday at 6:30 in the morning. And the temperature is . . . I could feel it coming and I didn't try to stop it. I just sat there, as the sky purpled and went white, and wept. For Hugo and Cindy Ann and Jo and me, who had killed that thing lying in the cabin like a dead fire.

The birds began to call among the trees. Jays and robins and the dark hoarse caw of a crow. I sat and waited. My eyes on the gravel road that wound through the trees. Waiting to hear the sound of the engine. To see the sun glint off those bull's horns. I held the pistol in my hand as I waited. Not a thought in my head. Too exhausted to think or plan.

At nine-ten I heard it. Heard it before I could see it through the trees. And I walked off the porch, swinging the whiskey bottle and the gun in either hand, and crouched down beside the east wall of the cabin, out of sight of the road.

The car was closer now. The tires scudding through the gravel, making a loose, sodden sound. And then the engine was so loud I wanted to hold my ears against it. And then it stopped.

The car door cracked open. And I could hear his feet on the dry ground.

"Rafe?" he called from below the porch. "Rafe?"

He started up the porch stairs and, suddenly, his foot turned to stone. The stair creaked as if he were rocking on it.

"Harry?" he said softly. "Boy, you in there?"

He had his gun out now.

"I'm comin' in," he shouted.

I crouched lower against the house, the white morning sunlight blazing in my eyes and the parsley curl of ailanthus cushioning my haunches and my back where the weed crawled among the struts beneath the cabin and up the cabin wall. I heard his footsteps on the porch, each one more tentative than the one before it, as he paced there in front of the door—his gun in one hand and the other hovering at the knob.

"Rafe?" he called again.

I edged closer to the porch, until I was below it, among the ailanthus and the sun-burst dandelions. Forcing myself to move at a crouch, biting my lips against the pain and the insane desire to shriek out to him, "Here, Red! Here I am!"

The planking above me creaked as he leaned toward the door. It wouldn't take him long, once he'd seen it. He'd be out again in a second, down the steps, and across the hard dirt yard to where the Cadillac sat winking in the sun. I waited for the sound of the door.

And, finally, it opened with a groan of splintering wood.

I pulled myself up, so that I was standing before the railing. I put the whiskey bottle down on the planks, braced myself with one arm, and extended my gun hand through the spindles—aiming at the open doorway.

There was a ghastly sound—as if the house itself were expelling its fetid breath. And I knew he'd seen him. Perhaps not believing what he'd seen at first. Not sure it was a human body. Then, walking over to it, as I had walked over to Preston LaForge's corpse—his own body electric with adrenaline. And when he'd seen it from close by, he'd gasped in horror and in the certainty that I was out there somewhere, waiting for him.

"Come on out, Red," I called from the porch. "Come on out, old man."

There wasn't a sound from inside the house.

"Come on *out!*" I screamed at the gaping door.

My own voice frightened me. I wasn't sure how much longer I could hold onto that ledge sanity, without blacking out or losing my grip entirely. Part of me already wanted to run screaming into the cabin, firing wildly as I ran.

But I made myself think of him, instead of me. I made myself picture him as he stood there beside Rafe. A light sweat on his creased face and in the prickle of hair upon his skull. Thinking as he would be thinking—that methodical cop's mind, sorting and discarding alternatives. He must have known I was hurt. How badly he couldn't tell. But he must have been wondering if he could wait me out. Just stand there until I keeled over in the sun. He'd heard my voice, heard the pain.

I had to do something to make him commit himself or he *could* wait me out, just as he was planning to do. I rubbed my hands across the rough porch planking and it came to me as if it were the one and only element in the universe.

The whole damn lodge was like a box of kindling. One spark and the wind would carry flames across the porch. Slowly, at first, maybe five minutes to get the fire going in earnest. Then the cabin would explode like ignited wood dust and take whatever was inside it up in a hot breathless gust.

I picked up the whiskey bottle and spilled what was left of the liquor on the planks. Then I lit my lighter and tossed it on the wood. A blue pool of fire swept the porch beneath the east railing, driving me back from the heat.

"You're going to burn, Red." I watched the flames creep along the boards, eating them away inch by inch. "You hear me? You're going to burn just like Rafe!"

The fire crackled and black smoke began to fill the overhang.

I stood back ten feet from the stoop and waited. He must have seen it by now. He had to have. The smoke was drifting through the doorway.

And then he called out. "Harry. I'm coming out. Hold your fire, son."

He pitched a revolver through the door, and it clattered down the steps.

"Don't shoot me, son. I ain't armed."

I raised the gun toward the door.

Out he came, swiping at the black smoke with his left hand and squinting against the heat. When he spotted me in the yard, his right arm jerked up. And I fired.

Red grabbed his chest with his left arm and fell

back against the door jamb, another gun clutched tightly in his right fist.

"Sweet Jesus!" he cried out. "You done killed me."

He slid slowly down the door jamb until he was sitting on the porch—his face was white, his chest overspread with blood, his gun lying in his hand. He breathed heavily.

Then he saw the flames as the fire swept toward him.

"Harry!" he shrieked, holding out a bloody hand. "Help me, son."

I just stood there and watched him watching the fire. It was up the north wall now, its yellow tongue licking at the door in which Bannion was lying.

"Harry!" he screamed again. "I'll burn alive!"

He looked at me—his face terrible in the smoke and the bright cast of the flames.

"Oh, my God!" he cried out.

He tried to move his legs, but they wouldn't work any more. He looked at me again, desperately and, with terrific effort, brought the gun in his right hand to his lips. Then pulled the trigger.

# 28

DOWN THOSE STONE steps in a little glen is where they found all that was left of Cindy Ann Evans. A piece of cloth with a blood stain on it, turned brown in the weather. And, in a lime pit, the shape of a smile, beside a shed used to store gear for men in the hunting lodge, her fleshless bones. Everything else burned away by the corrosive magnesium; and, with it, all that had fastened her to this world. All love and loyalty. All life.

The highway patrolmen found her. I wasn't there. Although I was well enough by then to go back out to the gutted cabin.

I had legitimate excuses—two broken ribs, my blistered hand, the place on my left cheek that had taken ten stitches to close, and the part of my skull that was concussed by that whiskey bottle and lacerated with glass. For five days I was one of the walking wounded. And for five days I had sat alone in a small county hospital north of Louisville, thinking of Jo. She never came. They called her when they brought me in to St. George's. I asked them to. But the days passed and I roamed the halls, scaring nurses with my bruised face—more than ever the face of a busted statue—and sitting in on card games with the invalided patients. Rummy and pinochle and cribbage. And she never came. They told me she called once on the first day, to make sure I was going to live. And, when, on the fifth day, with no pride left to swallow, I called the Busy Bee, Hank Greenberg told me she was gone.

"Where?" I asked him.

"I don't know, Harry. She called in on Saturday and said she was quitting. One of the girls drove by her place and the landlady told her that she'd left town."

"No forwarding address?"

"None."

And, so, on the sixth day, when they asked me if I wanted to go out to Corinth—which was the name of the little hamlet outside which the hunting lodge had been set—I begged off.

But all afternoon, in the slow heat of the white hospital corridors, I could see that lime pit in my mind's eye. And a part of me felt as if it, too, had plunged in and burnt away and, with it, a part of what held me to earth. I'd find her again, I told myself. After all, that's what I did for a living. Find things for people who'd lost them. I have a talent for it, like I'd said to her. Only sometimes things don't want to be found. People hide them away or destroy them. Then they're gone forever. And all that can be found is the place they once occupied, like those spaces in the magma at Pompeii where the hot lava settled around a tool or a dish and burned it away and then cooled so quickly that it took on the shape of the thing it destroyed. The thing itself . . . gone forever.

On the seventh day an officer with the highway patrol came to visit and, with him, Alvin Foster. They made an amusing pair. The one tall and military, shining with bright leather bandoliers and gold braid and sewn-on arm patches, with those ubiquitous aviator's glasses on his nose. And the other one, rumpled and shabby, reeking of tobacco, his flat ugly face morose and unsmiling.

"We just want to settle a few things, Mr. Stoner. For the record," the military one said. His name was Lee, and he acted like it. "Those two men you killed —there isn't any way on God's earth to prove that it didn't happen exactly as you said it did. Hell, from what we're finding out, they would've ended up dead one way or another." He straightened his glasses and seemed to squint at me as if he were looking at the sun through smoked glass. "Only it wasn't one way or another, was it? Lieutenant Foster, here, says you killed a man in Cincinnati. Self-defense, of course. That's the ruling, isn't it?"

Foster nodded.

"Sometimes a man's luck runs like that." He fidgeted with his glasses again and squinted hard. "But not in Franklin County," he said softly. "Not ever again. You understand?"

"Yeah," I said.

"Next time your business carries you across the river . . . well, just see that it doesn't. You understand?"

"I understand," I told him.

"Good." He seemed to relax a little, resting one hand on his gun butt and tucking the other in his belt. "We got Howie Bascomb under arrest. Of course, it's going to be tough to prosecute him for murder, unless the Jellicoes cooperate. But, I think they will. The husband is willing to plea-bargain if we drop the accessory to murder charge down to manslaughter. I think Calvin Young, our D.A., is willing to do that. Lord, I can't count the number of indictments that may eventually come out of this. Judge Stebbins over in Boone County. Alderman Russo in Newport."

I named the state senator whom Tray Leach had mentioned to me.

"Him, too," Lee said nervously. "You'll be called, of course, when trial dates are set." He glanced at Foster and said, "I guess that's all from my end."

Foster didn't say anything for a moment. Just stared at me speculatively, as if I was something new to his experience of men. "You've got guts, Stoner," he said, after a time. "I'll hand you that much. But, my God, man, you haven't got a brain in your head."

I laughed.

"It's not funny," he said. "Three dead men is nothing to laugh about. Will you please tell me one thing . . . why in hell didn't you cooperate with us? What the hell was worth so much risk?"

I looked away from his face. "She was," I said softly.

"Who?"

"The girl. Cindy Ann."

"Oh," he said with mild surprise. "The one in the lime pit."

"Yeah," I said. "The one everyone else wanted to hide."

On Thursday I caught a ride with a patrolman back to Newport and picked up my car in front of the theater.

"You know they found the owner of this place dead last week?" the cop said. "He was sitting in a seat in his theater, watching a film along with the other stiffs." He laughed at his own joke.

"Do they know why?"

"He had a lot of enemies," the cop said. "You know towns like this one are funny. I used to work in Vegas, so I know. You'd think in Newport that anything goes. But it ain't true. Open towns got their own code of morality."

"I guess that comes from looking out of one eye for too long."

The cop looked at me quizzically.

"And keeping the other one closed," I said.

"Oh, yeah," he said. "That's it, all right. No perspective."

He dropped me off by the marquee and I drove downtown to Charles Street and up to Porky Simlab's veranda. It was past noon and the gallery was full.

I walked up the front lawn and a burly young man I'd never seen before stopped me at the porch. He put a paw to my chest, like a Great Dane begging to be petted, and said, "Hold up, there, friend." He was a slick-looking kid, with just a touch of malice in his shiny blue eyes. With Red gone, I wondered how long Porky would last. This one had no loyalty in his face, at all.

"Tell Porky, Harry Stoner."

He looked at me a second and walked up to the veranda.

"You can come up," he called down after a minute.

Porky was in his easy chair. He had a black armband around his leisure suit, but, aside from that, he looked the same as ever.

"Hello, son," he said grimly.

"Porky."

"What you want around heah, *today?*"

"About Red . . ." I said. "I didn't have a choice."

"I figured."

I studied his fat farmboy's face. The pig-like eyes had gone dead when they saw me. Dead and old. "How about you, Porky? Did you have a choice?"

"Whachu mean, son?"

"You know what I mean, old man. There isn't much in this city that escapes your attention. You knew about Red. You just closed one eye and pretended you didn't see. For old time's sake, Porky? For an old friend?"

He didn't say anything for a second. Then he set his jaw and planted both stubby legs on the porch. "Don't come 'round heah, Harry. Don't come *back* no more, son."

The young tough ambled up behind me and Porky waved him back with his fat baby's hand and a wink of his mouth. "Won't be necessary, Lucius. The gen'lman's jus' *departing*."

"The joke is that he was afraid you'd find out. In a way, that's what got him killed."

Porky's face reddened. "*You* got him killed," he said flatly. "I won't forget it, neither."

I nodded to the kid behind me. "Better look out, Porky. If Red thought he could pull a buck out of your pocket while your back was turned, just think what that one is capable of."

He smiled like a baby jackal. "I'll keep it in mind."

And, maybe he would, I thought as I stepped off the porch. Anyone as affable as Porky Simlab has to be a predator at heart.

It was almost two when I parked the Pinto in the Jewish Hospital lot.

The receptionist in the lobby gave me his room number and asked me if I was a relative or a friend.

"A friend," I told her.

"Then you ought to know that he's in critical condition. He's been semi-comatose for almost a week. There isn't much chance that he'll live out the week."

I took a deep breath and let it out slowly. "Has he got . . . everything he needs?"

"His son's been in earlier this week, and I believe he's arranged a nurse for him."

I walked up to the second floor, where they keep the old ones with terminal illnesses. And down the hall, past the nurses station, where two pretty young nurses sat laughing behind the plexiglass window, to room two-ten.

He was sitting on the bed, staring blankly out the open window at the parking lot, where the cars were sparkling in the sun. He was wearing a thin hospital gown; his arms protruded from the sleeves like sticks. The blanket was folded neatly at his chest. There was no nurse in the room.

"Hello, Hugo."

He turned his head and looked up at me. Blankly. Then he smiled.

I walked over to the bed and squeezed his hand. He looked down at my hand the way a child looks at

**310**

a new rattle. Everything was new to him again. Every gesture and face. All new.

He looked up from my hand, cocked his wispy white head and tried to speak. He moved his mouth a couple of times. But the words that once filled it automatically wouldn't come, now. And he spent a second trying to figure out what had become of them, before he looked away with a trace of embarrassment in his juicy blue eyes.

I patted his hand again. "I found her, Hugo. She's fine."

He looked at me uncertainly.

"Cindy Ann is fine," I said. "She was in Denver. Like I thought. I found her and sent her home to Sioux Falls."

Something connected in Hugo's shattered mind. His eyes filled with tears and his thin lips trembled. He touched my hand.

"I gave her your love," I said heavily.

My throat began to burn. "She told me she loved you, too."

He tried to say something again. His mouth struggled with the thought, but no words came out.

━━━━━

There was a check from Meyer on my anteroom floor. And a note from Jo postmarked almost a week before. I tucked the note in my coat pocket and walked into the inner office.

The wasps were at it, again.

I put my feet up on the desk and stared at them and thought about Hugo Cratz.

I didn't think he'd believed me—about Cindy Ann.

But, then, Hugo was always a hard man to lie to. And she was all he'd had.

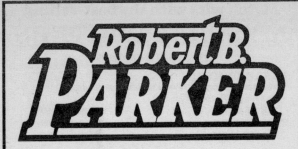